NEVER HIT A JELLYFISH
WITH A SPADE

GUY BROWNING writes the 'How to' column in the *Guardian* 'Weekend' magazine. He is also a business consultant specializing in creativity. He lives quietly in Oxfordshire.

My thanks to...
Lisa Darnell, Kate Jones, Toby Mundy, Louisa Joyner,
Katharine Viner, David Christensen, Dave Belcher,
Ross Woodford and the great Graeme Wilkinson for
their inspiration and professionalism.

Most of all thanks to Esther for going easy
with the spade.

Contents

SPORT AND EXERCISE

How to... exercise

They say the devil makes work for idle hands. He also makes work for other parts of the body and this he calls exercise. By exercise we mean any kind of movement you wouldn't normally make in everyday life. However, everyday movements can be converted into exercise by adding the word 'power': hence 'power walking', 'power lifting' and 'power dressing'. There are two types of exercise – aerobic and anaerobic. Aerobic exercise is what you do in Lycra, anything else is anaerobic.

Exercise is good for you in all sorts of ways. The fitter you are, the more you can do things like climb stairs and run for a bus – in other words, other forms of exercise. After a really strenuous workout, you get a great feeling of well-being. This is due to the release of endorphins into the bloodstream, which are the body's natural smugness generators.

The best part of exercising is sweating. This cleans all the pores and allows you to use sports body wash instead of just soap. Sweating also makes you look like a great steaming mess and explains why exercise itself is very uncool and only becomes cool once you've cooled off, showered down and emerged with slightly wet hair.

It's very easy to get addicted to exercise. You can become so fit that you push yourself to ever-greater extremes, one of which is death. People who are always out exercising generally carry a subliminal message on their sweatshirt: 'rubbish relationship'.

Nowadays there are all sorts of machines that simulate exercise for you. For example, there are running machines, ski machines and rowing machines. Ideally, they would have a remote control so you could operate them while you sat on the sofa watching TV. Normally, exercise machines tend to end up in the spare room because that's where you put stuff you don't use.

Exercise is a great way to lose weight, principally because it's hard to eat a tub of ice cream while you're doing aqua-aerobics. Yoga devotees say it's the toughest form of exercise in that you can lift the equivalent of half a ton just by clenching your buttock muscles. People who get really good at yoga can put their leg behind their head. However, it generally takes another year of practice before you can get it back.

One of the great benefits of regular exercise is that you develop a superb body. Ideally, this becomes a smoothly oiled love machine. Except for the fact that no one wants to sleep with anyone who breaks off to take on board high-energy liquids during lovemaking and has to do fifteen minutes of stretching before starting.

How to... use a changing room

A changing room is halfway between a meeting room and a bathroom. It's the only place where you have to be businesslike and naked at the same time.

Communal showers have two temperatures: glacial or scalding. Standing at one side with your hand in the shower will not significantly alter the temperature either way. At the very least, you can tilt your head into the shower for two seconds, keeping your body well clear, in order to give your hair the just-showered look vital for the bar afterwards.

It's important to wash your private bits in the shower, but they must only be given a brisk buffing. Anything more leisurely will be seen as indulgence bordering on wanton self-gratification. Once out of the shower you should dry yourself immediately. Promenading with arms akimbo is a big no-no. At the other extreme, some people do their best to dry themselves as much as possible inside their locker. Others wrap a towel round their waist and then try to pass all their clothes up underneath.

There are two places you are allowed to look in a

changing room: the floor and the ceiling. You are also allowed to look in the mirror, but only to give your hair a once-through with a comb. Hours in front of the mirror bouffing up your hair up will undo any amount of heroic performance on the sports field/exercise bicycle.

In a communal shower you should not stand face-out as this would be considered grotesque exhibitionism, nor should you stand facing in as this suggests you have something to hide. You should stand 45–115° off-centre and then lather yourself until you're covered head to foot in a wall of suds. Take one bottle of body wash into the shower and one bottle only. Avoid bringing your own bar of soap from home in a plastic soap-dish. If you drop your soap at any time, leave it. Don't go back for it. Simply rinse quickly and leave smartly.

It is imperative never to speak to anyone in the changing room ever, unless you have lost a limb or are attempting to evacuate the building. An occasional 'Sorry' is fine if you've accidentally put your shoes on someone's bit of bench. Never follow up with 'My goodness, your buttocks have left a big wet patch on the bench.'

Some changing rooms have communal baths where the whole team can soak and have a chat. Remember, entry to a communal bath is by invitation only, so don't attempt to slip in when there is a full team of rugby players already ensconced.

How to... be in a team

In life you're either a team player or someone who doesn't get picked for teams. Loners and rugged individualists have usually chosen their lifestyle because they were sick of it being chosen for them at school.

Every team must have a captain. This is always the person who has the most success with the opposite sex. Only someone with this track record has the natural authority to pick a team. The first people to be selected are the captain's best mates, followed by people who have sporting prowess. Last to be selected are people who turn up conscientiously but have the ball control of a toddler.

Once on the pitch, the various elements of the team become clear. The shouter is the most obvious one. This is a person who sees almost nothing of the ball throughout the entire match, possibly because the ball doesn't like shouting. The shouter will give continuous loud instructions about where the ball should be placed – for example, down the wing, through the middle, on the shouter's head. This gives the opposition a very clear idea of where the ball won't be going.

The person with talent in the team soon becomes apparent. They will do something with real skill and dexterity before being stretchered off after a freak incident involving assault by eleven members of the other team with hockey sticks (especially nasty in a netball match).

No team is complete without its kit. Responsibility for washing the kit is given to the person most desperate to be in the team. In rugby teams washing the kit is often an initiation rite as getting the exact amount of fabric conditioner right can be tricky.

A vital part of team sport is the communal bath or shower. That's why it's essential to have decent-sized equipment unless for some reason you're a woman. The showers are where you begin to celebrate your great victory or forget your epic defeat. In both scenarios, the emotional purging is aided by rolled towels being whipped smartly across the underpants area of other team members.

It's worth remembering that your standing in the team can be seriously undermined if you take more than one bottle into the shower. If you must take two bottles, make sure one is a premium German lager.

You won't get far as a team player unless you can sing on the coach. Team songs can have three possible themes: the sexual potency of the singers, the sexual inadequacy of the opposition, or the private life of animals. Often these themes are delicately interwoven. The ability to make up verses of uncommon obscenity can guarantee a permanent place in the team.

How to... do extreme sports

Extreme sports all boil down to thinking up great new ways of killing yourself and then extracting the death part at the last moment. Anything that gives you the experience of a roller-coaster without the roller-coaster itself can be classified as an extreme sport.

All extreme sports aspire to free fall. Take extreme skiing, or ski extreme as it's sometimes called. Here you ski down slopes that are technically precipices and that would require ropes and crampons to come up the other way. Really extreme ski extreme extremists do away with skis and slopes altogether and just throw themselves out of a helicopter somewhere cold. They do some hotdogging on the way down and, if things go wrong, do something called the hamburger, which is when they hit concrete at terminal velocity.

You can measure the extremeness of your sport by the safety equipment you carry: cycle helmet and knee pads and you might as well be playing extreme bingo; ropes and harness and the risk level goes up; life jackets always look good, but to really impress you either need a parachute or an ejector seat. Ideally, your dangerous sport should require a combination of ejector seat, life jacket, parachute, ropes, harness and knee pads. Of course, some people go rambling kitted out like this in order to give the impression that they're doing something risky. The impression they give is that they're an extreme idiot.

White-water rafting is very similar to having a cold shower while someone tries to shove a twelve-man dinghy into your cubicle. White-water rafting can be made more extreme by having half the water in the form of rocks. For an extra frisson you can also add hippopotami, who hate nothing more than have their bathing disturbed by a twelve-man dinghy landing on their heads. Bungee jumping was invented by antipodeans who thought jumping off a bridge was too much fun to be left to potential suicides.

It's vital if you're going to do any kind of extreme sport to dress like you're a surf dude and to shout 'Whoaaaaaa!!!' when you're doing it. Turning up in a comfortable tweed jacket and doing something extreme while whistling nonchalantly just makes everyone else feel as though they're wasting their time.

The big secret with extreme sports is that they're all rather easy. That's because all extreme sports are gravity-assisted. No one classes ultra-marathon running or single-handed circumnavigation or Arctic crossings as extreme sports because they require monumental effort, discipline and strength. Besides which you'd freeze your nads off in surf gear and nobody would hear you going 'Whoaaaaaa!!!' when you disappeared down a ninety-foot crevasse.

How to... run a marathon

Occasionally you'll see people doing a strange sport called backwards stair-climbing. This is what happens the day after you've run a marathon because you've got hamstrings longer than a double bass.

Dressing correctly is vital for a marathon and everything should be chosen to maximize cooling and minimize energy loss. Which is why, if you're plodding round in your high-tech, high-cost running gear, it's incredibly galling when someone roars past dressed in a six-foot chicken costume and carrying a bucket of loose change.

Getting water on board is vitally important and most people drink many pints before they even start. This, combined with the very real excitement at the beginning of the race, means that shortly after the start you have about ten thousand people stopping for a pee. Strangely, they never show this on the TV. On the way round, don't make the mistake of thinking that you can pick up water on the run. You can't pick up your tea at home on the run, so don't try it during a race: you'll just end up soaking yourself and then, when you try and drink it on the move, you'll spend five minutes choking yourself to death.

During the race liquids are vital, but not solids – which is why you have mixed feelings about kindly spectators who hold out sweets, toasted sandwiches and traditional Sunday roasts. If your body does run out of energy, you hit something called the wall. This happens at around twenty miles (or earlier if you don't look where you're going). The wall is where you start burning parts of your body that are normally left for furnishing – like fat and muscle. There is another bit that starts to get burnt away, and that is your will to live. Which is why during the first twenty miles of a marathon you can enjoy the scenery and the last six miles are like running in a small cupboard marked 'pain'.

At the end of a marathon you're generally so whacked you decide not to lift your arms at the finishing line because it involves too much energy. There's usually an automatic photo taken of you crossing the line and the expression on your face is probably the closest you'll ever get to seeing what you look like first thing in the morning. Then the sense of physical achievement sets in and you can start telling everybody what a supreme physical specimen you are (as long as they aren't upstairs).

How to... swim

Many people who can't swim pretend to do so by splashing around vigorously but at the same time keeping one foot on the bottom. You might be able to get away with this in the municipal swimming baths, but not with the surfing crowd at Malibu.

The first stroke most people master is the doggy-paddle. You would have thought people would start with the fish-paddle because fish are generally better role models when it comes to swimming. But then we're odd like that – we also try to swim like a butterfly, which is actually better known for flying.

Once you're in, you have a choice of strokes. Backstroke is where you lie on your back and just at the point of sinking you throw your arms back and make like a paddle steamer. You do this until you do a full-power reverse karate chop on the concrete side of the pool and decide that swimming on your front might be more sensible. Again, you won't find many fish swimming on their backs unless they're dead.

With breaststroke you can choose to do it either with your head out of the water or dipping under. If you choose to dip and you haven't come up after the third dip, the technical name for what you're doing is drowning. Sidestroke is for people who, given a horse, would ride side saddle. It's actually a very efficient stroke but it does give the impression that you're having a prolonged ogle at anyone swimming alongside you.

There are two types of front crawl: there's the controlled application of power as done by Australians; and then there's the crawl done by British men, which involves one length at maximum effort, beating the hell out of the water, creating more wake than a passing car ferry, and knocking unconscious any other swimmer who happens to be in the way.

You can combine various strokes into the individual medley: this is where you start with something impressive like crawl or butterfly, swallow half the swimming pool, and then do a few strokes of something else like breaststroke while you fight for air and try to stop choking.

The one area where the British excel in the swimming pool is headgear – especially the rubber helmets with flowers stuck on them favoured by older women and designed for covert operations in lily ponds. These helmets are worn by a certain kind of lady who drifts aimlessly around the pool like a Portuguese man-of-war on a spring tide. Look at these women closely and you'll notice they've generally got one foot on the bottom.

How to... ride a horse

Imagine you were just minding your own business when a small primate landed on your back and demanded to go somewhere. That's how a horse feels when you decide to ride it.

One of the first things you'll notice about a horse is that it has twice the number of legs we do and therefore bounces up and down in a different way from us when it moves. The American response to this is to have a saddle like a comfy old armchair and then to slump well down in it. The British response has been to develop a saddle like a panty liner and then keep the bottom well clear of it as if it were red hot.

Horses go in two directions: towards food and away from food. They also have two speeds: fast and slow. They move slowly away from food and fast towards it. Reins are the gearstick of a horse. Holding them loosely in your hands is neutral, pulling on them lightly is forward, and yanking roughly on them is eject.

For the first-time rider, the most shocking thing about a horse is the complete absence of a handle. This means you can't steer and you can't hold on. Incredibly, what you're supposed to do is to steer and hold on with your knees and inner thighs. Which is why making love to an experienced horsewoman feels a lot like spending the night in a Corby trouser press.

By law you have to wear a helmet when you ride. Riding helmets have been designed to offer complete protection should you fall off your horse, execute a perfect twisting pike turn and land upright on the crown of your head. Landing any other way will give you massive concussion and cause you intermittent black-outs for seventy-two hours afterwards. This kind of fall is known as a three-day eventer.

Once people get on horses they feel the need to jump things. Horses don't naturally jump things, otherwise the corral would have been a pretty rubbish invention. Can you imagine how little the horse thinks of its rider when on either side of the eight-foot fence is a perfectly good way of moving towards food without the need for jumping?

Stirrups are an integral stepladder designed to help you mount a horse. If you put a foot in, swing up and can't see the horse's head, you're probably on back-wards. Don't be embarrassed by this as tests have shown that rear-facing riders suffer significantly fewer injuries in a crash. You're also less likely to jump things in this position and more likely to find horse food quickly.

How to... win at sports day

Children, the time to start training for school sports day is now. Winning is everything. Your parents may have taken a day off work to see you run and they don't want to see you limping in at the back of the field. Remember, your mummy or daddy may have sacrificed a very important meeting that would have helped pay the mortgage on the house in which your bedroom and toys are.

In the sprint you can't just run really fast anywhere – you have to run in between those white lines. Why? Because the International Olympic Committee say so, that's why. If halfway up the course all the other children are in front of you, it really doesn't matter where you run because mummy and daddy won't be hanging around at the finishing line if that's your attitude.

In the egg and spoon race the object is to get to the finishing post with your egg still in your spoon, not to see how many times you can drop it and pick it up. Other parents may find this cute and funny; yours won't, and they're the ones with the keys to the front door. Refereeing is often lax, even non-existent in this event.

You won't have time to glue your egg to your spoon but you can pick a spoon with greater concavity than the others. Ask your mother for a soup ladle if possible. When you find yourself neck and neck with other kids, simply put your thumb on your egg and run a bit faster. No one's going to ask for a stewards' inquiry because you're only a kid and you don't know any better.

Children who are not naturally athletic are advised to focus on the three-legged race. Avoid teaming up with your best friend Timothy: he may have great toys but in the coordination department he's a bit of a dork. Pick someone with the same leg length as you and then walk quickly to school with them for the rest of term until lockstep becomes second nature. If you're the big porky boy in the class, pick the weediest boy in your class to run with. Don't worry about his stride pattern or anything else. Just drag him along as fast as you can go. If you've tied your knots right, he will still be there at the finishing line.

School sports days often have a parents' race. This is different from kids' races and is not competitive. When your daddy comes seventh or eighth that is good. The other adults were in too much of a hurry and were probably showing off. If you have won your race and your daddy hasn't, don't mention sports day for a few weeks.

How to... climb a tree

Climbing trees has become a bit of a forgotten art. The only time you see someone up one is when they are cutting it down or trying to prevent it being cut down. Children wouldn't think of climbing a tree unless it was a fully interactive computer game featuring Gonad the Larchslayer.

It's important to pick the right tree to climb. No one's going to be very impressed if you attempt to climb a tree that is shorter than you are. Similarly, be careful of odd-shaped trees. If you just steam in and start climbing a weeping willow you'll find that the more you climb, the closer you get to the ground. Also, there are no prizes for climbing thick conifers. Only attempt a conifer if you can see a clear benefit in having your clothes shredded and your skin flayed.

Pick a stout, deciduous, broadleaf tree, about forty to fifty feet high, which could comfortably accommodate Robin Hood and at least five Merry Men. Then start the most difficult bit of all, which is getting into the tree. There are no easy routes up trees, otherwise you'd see deer and cows grazing in them.

To get yourself started, you have to jump up and grab a low-hanging branch and then either walk up the tree or fling your legs up. Once you're in, the rest is plain sailing. The tricky bit is knowing when to stop climbing: swaying is caution, snapping is stop, and blue sky above the ankle is intensive care unit.

If you've only ever climbed a rope before, be aware that it's not the same action. You can't hold a tree between your feet and push up. If you can, you've either got monstrous feet or you're halfway up someone's washing line.

One of the big problems about climbing trees is what to do once you're at the top. If there's a view, that's lovely, and you can look at that. But if you've done it to impress your mates, they are now a long way below and have probably gone home for their tea. Remember, you may feel you're three hundred feet up but from where they're standing it doesn't look very impressive. Unless you're wearing a kilt.

Tree houses are where you get all the benefits of climbing a tree without the problems of being up it. But remember that nailing planks to a tree is actually rather insensitive as it's not dissimilar to asking a cow to wear a leather jacket. There are two traditional ways of coming down a tree: one is lowering your legs down in great big groin-stretching slithers; the other is the fire brigade.

How to... ramble

One of the unintended consequences of cutbacks in rail services has been the relentless rise in rambling. When there are few trains to spot, dull people start walking around aimlessly and inevitably start rambling.

Ramblers have boiled sweets in flavours so repulsive you'd rather eat your own leg in an emergency situation. They wear high-tech anoraks that wick heat and moisture away from their bodies and release it into the noses of other ramblers. Ramblers have big boots. This is to stop them falling over when they've had their second pint of real ale at the end of their epic four-mile ramble.

Ramblers travel in packs and are always led by a man or woman with a beard and a big knobbly stick. He's known as Ramblo. Ramblers have maps in perspex holders (so they won't get soaked by all the moisture being wicked away from their bodies). With these detailed maps and large compasses they can work out that they're three hundred yards from the car park.

Ramblers engage in conversation when they walk, and it's no surprise that they tend to ramble. In any pack of ramblers you'll have someone who knows a bit about birds, someone who knows a bit about plants, and someone who knows a bit about soils. The upshot of this is that you can't move five yards without one of them piping up with a half-hour lecture on the fascinating Kimmeridge clays that everyone's big boots are currently sinking into.

Ramblers love unspoilt countryside, and sometimes you can spot great packs of brightly coloured ramblers grinding through the country getting the maximum enjoyment from it. Ramblers think that the best way of seeing the country is to walk directly behind some achingly dull cagouled idiot for six hours.

You can always tell a rambler because they're dressed for the Himalayas. They're the ones carrying the emergency bivouac, Primus stove and distress flares on the Thames towpath. Long-distance paths do a great service to society by keeping ramblers in remote parts of the country for extended periods and well away from normal people.

The right to roam would be so much more palatable if you could guarantee that the first person to traipse across your lawn wouldn't be a rambler. No one likes people rambling when they're talking, so why should we put up with it when people walk. If you want to get somewhere, fine, but for Pete's sake don't ramble. Ramblers should be hunted by horse and hound. That would get them moving.

SICKNESS AND HEALTH

How to... sneeze

Sneezing is an enormously powerful bodily convulsion second only to the orgasm in its intensity. Both are difficult to fake with any degree of accuracy, and it's best not to attempt either in a lift unless you are by yourself or with someone who loves you a very great deal.

There are many different ways to stop sneezing. The most common is to put a finger under your nose and push up. Alternatively you can push your tongue against the back of your teeth. Do both together and you also get a passable imitation of a member of the aristocracy.

Sneezing expels air from your nose at approximately 100 mph, except in Norfolk where it's much slower. Were it possible to suspend a miniature wind turbine from the nose, the energy of an average sneeze would be sufficient to power a small reading light for long enough to find your handkerchief. If you feel you're about to sneeze, you should always turn your head so that instead of spattering the person you're speaking to with spittle, mucus and bits of cabbage, you create an interesting collage effect on their wall.

Sneezes are divided into the Ah and the Choo. Some people do the sneezing on the Ah, others on the Choo. In general, the amount of noise you make sneezing is a direct reflection of your performance in bed. A huge great trumpeting noise means it's good news in the duvet department, while an annoying little 'phit' means precious little headboard activity.

Occasionally a sneeze will let you know it's coming with a tickling sensation in the nose. This makes you screw up your eyes and take a little sequence of short breaths. Often as not, nothing then happens and you put your handkerchief back in your pocket. That's when the sneeze arrives, delivering half a pound of A-grade phlegm onto the lapel of a visiting dignitary. You can sometimes bring reluctant sneezes on by staring into lights. Don't try this when you're driving as you may get a powerful and satisfying sneeze but it will be your last one ever.

'Sneeze' is a very interesting word. The slower version of sneeze is snooze, where the air moves much slower. Where the air is totally stationary in the nose, the sneeze becomes a snot. You'll notice that some people have a double-barrelled sneeze. Research has been conducted into whether this is because one sneeze comes from each nostril. No results were obtained because the researchers kept getting ill.

When other people sneeze, the traditional response is to say 'Bless you', which is derived from 'God bless you'. It is quite acceptable for atheists to substitute 'General humanitarian benefits to you'.

How to... have a cold

Having a cold is like winter taking up residence in your body, without the skiing. People who don't have a cold dismiss it as a minor irritation. People who have a cold tend to view it as the same virus that wiped out the Aztec empire. Like margarine, colds spread very easily. Most often the germs are passed on by touch, so it's best to avoid shaking hands and instead revert to other methods of greeting – for example, by fax.

The British are renowned for their phlegm, and during a full-blown cold the average nose will produce phlegm equivalent to half your body weight. It's a sobering thought that the salient British characteristic is what you've just deposited in your handkerchief.

Of all the nasty things you can pick up these days, a cold is relatively minor. However, the amateur dramatics it gives rise to are spectacular. Horrific wasting diseases that confine you to bed mean that people have to actively seek you out in order to sympathize. A cold, on the other hand, is a portable complaint. Not only can you take it to someone, you can give it to them to prove just how bad it really is.

There is a saying that 'coughs and sneezes spread diseases'. To prevent this you should sneeze into your hand. Never examine the contents of your hand immediately after sneezing into it, especially if your head is still joined to your hand by a long bridge of snot.

The enemy of the cold is the hot toddy. This is a traditional remedy consisting of whisky, honey, nutmeg, paraffin, WD-40, and the juice of a lemon. A properly made hot toddy is so disgusting to drink that the cold seems relatively pleasant afterwards.

To clear a runny nose, put a finger to one nostril and blow smartly out of the other. This is often frowned upon, generally by the person next to you covered head to foot in phlegm. Putting a towel over your head and inhaling steam can also clear the passages. Just be careful that while you're under the towel someone else doesn't clear your flat. Most people clear their nose by blowing into a tissue. Women often stuff this tissue up their sleeves. When they have really bad colds they can end up stuffing so much paper up their sleeves that they look like a female Schwarzenegger.

Just about the only consolation for having a cold is the lovely deep husky voice that goes with it. Sadly, because a cold also makes your brain hurt, you tend to use this new voice to talk deep, husky self-pitying rubbish. Interestingly, the voice is at its most husky on the telephone, especially when explaining your absence to colleagues at work.

How to... have flu

Flu goes through very clear stages. The first is when you suspect you have a temperature and ask someone to feel your forehead. In normal life we don't go around feeling people's foreheads, so it's often surprising how warm they are. Thankfully, few people will ask you to feel their nose and ask if it's runny.

To have flu you need symptoms; the standard ones are headache, sore throat, temperature, sickness, achiness, cough and dribbly nose. Once you've got four out of seven you can skip work. A cough must sound as though you're starting a chainsaw in cold weather, and you must cough at least three times on the phone during any conversation with work. Saying you've just got a temperature isn't good enough; you've got to have a raging fever of 120°. Clogged mucal sniffing is also good on the phone, but don't try to communicate general achiness or you may come across as a bit of a ham.

Stage two is bed. Once you're in bed with flu you need to accessorize. A large box of tissues is vital, as is the little hailstorm of used tissues around the bin where you haven't quite got the energy to throw them in. You'll also need some paracetamol to cope with the symptoms of flu. One of the nastiest symptoms is the headache and vomiting shortly after having the hot toddy specially prepared for you by someone who claims to love you.

You normally lose your appetite when you have flu, so if you find yourself eating a lot of cake and ice cream you're more likely to be pregnant. There's a saying 'feed a cold, starve a fever', or 'starve a cold, feed a fever'. Neither makes much sense. These sayings are used by elderly relatives as an excuse to give you the country soup they make by feeding compost into a blender and which 'will have you on your feet in no time'. You'll certainly be on your feet, but you'll just be running quickly for the lavatory.

The final phase of flu is the hacking cough, where you feel much better but you still sound like death. Use this time to get maximum attention and pampering and to make more deathbed phone calls to work. Finally, go back to work fit and ready, and realize that the people you thought were doing your work for you while you were away have also been off with flu.

How to... see the doctor

Before you get to see the doctor you generally have to sit in the waiting room. After fifty minutes you discover the reason behind the term 'patient'. However, waiting does give you time to look at all the other malingerers. Unless someone has clearly got a saucepan wedged on their head, there's always the suspicion that they're just wasting the doctor's valuable time which would be far better spent on your life-threatening rash. Waiting rooms are often decorated with informative posters. It can be quite unsettling to see old Mrs Mimms sitting quietly under a poster which says 'STDs – Coming to a Groin Near You'.

When you finally see the doctor they will give you a quick glance to check for obvious saucepan-on-head syndrome and then ask you how you are. This isn't small talk and you shouldn't reply with 'Mustn't grumble'. It's the green light to let rip with all the hundreds of symptoms your partner has been gleefully pooh-poohing for months.

You will then be asked a supplementary question by the doctor along the lines of 'Does it hurt more when you sit?' They already know what's wrong with you – they're just trying to give the impression of canny medical sleuthing to track down the sources of your mysterious cold. Only be worried if they start leafing through thick textbooks and consulting horrific-looking colour charts.

Whatever's wrong with you, the doctor will get their stethoscope out or test your blood pressure. They use the stethoscope when they can't stand you talking any more, and blood pressure testing has the same effect as someone taking you firmly by the arm and giving you a good talking-to. When the doctor says your pressure's normal, it then seems rather churlish to bring up the subject of your smashed ribs and collapsed lung.

The most intimidating person in the surgery is the receptionist. She has a photographic memory and when you call for an appointment she will remember your notes and know that you are a serial waster of NHS resources with your intermittent fungal infections.

There is one doctor in every surgery who is a bit of a dud. You can see them at any time, night or day. Or you can equally well take a couple of aspirin and see yourself again in a couple of weeks if your typhoid hasn't cleared up.

In the waiting room, patients will be called every thirty seconds for the doctor you're not seeing. After about an hour and a half a patient will finally come out from your doctor and you will ask yourself what he's got that you haven't. The answer is probably private medical insurance.

How to... keep your dentist happy

Keeping dentists happy can be a bit of a job because they all tend to be a bit down in the mouth.

First thing to do is to brush regularly, but not with that gnarled old toilet brush you're using. Whatever toothbrush you have, it's entirely inadequate for the job and is doing untold damage each time you pop it in your mouth. What you really need is one with a bendy handle, angled head, contoured bristles and textured grip, which you can buy in reception.

Second, make sure you floss before you go to bed every night – ignoring for the moment the fact that anyone who finds time to floss every night isn't really alive. Count the number of romantic novels that include the phrase 'Just before dawn they fell into bed after flossing.'

Don't eat Hungarian goulash with added garlic the night before you see your dentist unless you fancy a punitive strike on your wisdom teeth. Similarly, when you rinse, remember there is a little bowl to spit into. You'd be amazed at the number of people who go the wrong way and soak the dental hygienist.

Never ask dentists why they went into dentistry, as the

very clear subtext of this question is, 'How can you spend your life looking into people's mouths and up their nostrils?' It's best that you say nothing because one of the big reasons they went into dentistry is the opportunity to talk to people about their passion for collecting bricks with no danger that the person will run away or even attempt to talk back. If you do attempt to change the subject of conversation, don't be surprised if you're suddenly given a local anaesthetic.

Dentists have a big downer on chocolate, sweets and all forms of sugar. They would rather you lived off water, tree bark and grubs, which are all good for teeth and gums. Dentists would also like you a lot better if you had dislocatable jaws like a python. You can never open quite wide enough for a dentist as there's always a tooth somewhere in the back of your head that needs poking. Similarly, it's best to grow up without wisdom teeth as there's something about these little fellers that really upsets dentists.

If you don't want to see your dentist so much, become friends with your hygienist. This doesn't mean taking her chocolates and bags of sugar. It means flossing and brushing on a regular basis, gnawing tree bark, and wearing orthodontic braces that look like an early prototype for an American football helmet.

How to... have a sight test

When your optician asks you to get into the chair, make sure it doesn't tilt back and have a little bowl to rinse in, because whatever happens in that chair, it won't help your eyesight. All it tells you is that you were absolutely right to think that you needed glasses.

Once you've found the chair, the optician will slip a pair of heavy metal glasses on you that look like they've been knocked together by the local blacksmith. Whatever your optician tells you, this is not the latest look in Notting Hill nor are they the new National Health style. They are for test purposes only and you should not find yourself wearing them home under any circumstances.

The sight test itself starts when they ask you what the lowest line on the eye chart is. Don't waste their time by saying 'Printed in the UK'. Your best bet is to say 'What eye chart?' or even to look startled and say 'Who's there?' The optician will then slide a number of frames into your special metal glasses and keep asking you whether it's better with this one or with that one. This is a huge optician's wind-up as they're all exactly the same.

They just want a bit more time to laugh at you in your big metal glasses.

Remember, the phrase opticians hate most in this test is 'They're much of a muchness.' Say this once too often and they will send you away with a pair of glasses that make you see round corners and, when you complain, they'll say that all glasses are much of a muchness. Opticians also like to ask whether the circles are clearer in the red box or in the green box. This is no time to tell them that you're colour-blind (otherwise it's the blacksmith's glasses for you).

At some stage the optician will want to take a closer look at your eyes. They will then ask you to put your chin in a little holder and approach you as if it was their first snog. While they're staring into your eyes it's important to maintain eye contact. If you look away or blink, it's the blacksmith's glasses for you. During this stage you get the unpleasant impression that your entire skull is empty and the optician is thinking, 'My God, there's absolutely nothing in there!'

Finally, you'll walk out of the shop with your glasses and crystal-clear vision and suddenly see that your job, home and family are nothing like you'd imagined. And all everyone else thinks is 'Why is he wearing those big metal glasses?'

How to... eat healthily

Some day in your life you are going to have to look a prune full in the face and decide that it is good for you and that it should go in your mouth. This is the moment when you become more concerned about dying from natural causes than from unnatural causes.

If it's true that you are what you eat, then Britain is currently raising a large population of chicken nuggets. The general rule is that people come to resemble the food they eat. Habitual kebab eaters often become lumps of tasteless fat that can occasionally be extremely dangerous. There is also a moral dimension in diet: vegetarians choose not to eat meat or fish, while vegans don't eat any animal products. Real fanatics refuse to eat anything natural whatsoever and instead buy frozen ready meals.

Top government scientists advise us to eat five portions of fruit and veg every day. This gives the impression that you should really be loitering around a greengrocer's barrow for most of the daylight hours. But if you look at the rules carefully you find that one 'portion' is actually the equivalent of a slice of lemon in your gin and tonic or a few licks of a strawberry Mivvi.

There are some vitamins that your body produces naturally. For example, you can get vitamin D from sunlight, so spending the entire summer in Britain gives you your recommended daily allowance once. These days, vitamins are added to everything from lip gloss to floor polish. In fact, the only place where you won't find any added supplements is in organic fruit and veg, so it's probably best to steer clear of them.

Roughage is an essential part of any healthy diet, principally because it keeps everything moving south. In order to guarantee one bowel movement a day, scientists recommend a daily intake of roughage equivalent to the construction of a mid-sized Canadian beaver dam. Muesli is good roughage, but even here there are grades of healthiness. If you're eating it from a box you're still only flirting with muesli. You really need to be eating it from a bag or, better still, making your own from household and garden waste.

Given the choice, kids always plump for the least healthy option. This gives parents an excuse for the rest of their lives to say, 'You could have been a genius/ model/Olympian if only you'd eaten your spinach.' Strangely, as you get older you eat more and more unpleasant things that are supposedly good for you. When your diet is 90 per cent dried fruit and prunes you know it's time either to die or to switch to chicken nuggets and live a little.

How to... do first aid

First aid is where you try to remember what you did for your Cub badge before somebody dies in your arms. The thing to remember is that if you want to get people to recover it's vital to get them into the recovery position. This is the same position men adopt when recovering from sex. Women's recovery position from sex is much the same as their position preparing for sex, i.e. nightie down, crossword up.

The next thing to do is to check whether the airways are blocked. Do this by asking quickly but firmly, 'Are your airways blocked?' If they answer you'll know that their airways are clear. At the same time you can pick up valuable information about their condition – for example, if their response is 'Of course they're not blocked, I've broken my ankle.'

If you get no reply, you can check their breathing by holding a mirror in front of their face. Don't use one of those heavy, gilt-framed monsters as these can fall on top of the injured person and crush them. Use a small pocket mirror and then look closely at it. If all you can see are your own nostrils, then you've got it upside down. Turn the mirror round and check for telltale condensation on the mirror. This is a sure-fire method of telling whether the patient is condensing.

In the case of bleeding, a well-tied tourniquet is vital. Rip off the hem of your petticoat and tie it tightly around the wound. Remember, most people bleed to death because of the delay in finding someone with a petticoat. Tie the tourniquet on the side of the wound nearest the heart. If you're not sure which side this is, then tie tourniquets above, below and anywhere else that looks useful. The overall effect should be that the patient looks like they're about to go morris dancing.

Artificial resuscitation is based on male teenage behaviour in cinemas. Start with a lot of mouth-to-mouth but preferably without too much tongue. Then move on to a series of continuous heavy lunges at the chest area. Finally, attach electrodes and give them a series of massive electric shocks (teenagers don't actually do this last phase in cinemas).

Generally, accident victims should not be moved until an ambulance arrives. However, you may find yourself in an area without good transport links, i.e. Britain. Prepare a basic splint from two sturdy bits of wood, shove the limb in quite forcefully and then lash it up really tight. The whole body can be immobilized in this fashion if required. If things take a turn for the worst, you can then put a lid on the whole lot and dig them in for a convenient burial.

How to... prevent choking

Choking is like being strangled from inside. It's no laughing matter, even though it can sound very much like a laughing matter to begin with. If you're prone to this kind of thing it's best to steer well clear of jewellery, especially chokers, choke chains, throttlers, etc.

When you see someone choking the first thing you should attempt to do is remove the invoice from the plumber from their hand. This should do the trick, but if they are still in difficulty you could try the Heimlich manoeuvre. This is named after a famous World War One German ace who would put his plane through a serious of violent barrel rolls, stall turns and inverted loops in order to dislodge errant bits of sausage. Simply apply these manoeuvres to the chokee and all will be well.

If this fails you should move on to the Rorschach test. This is basically a test where you look at an ink-spot and decide what it is. It's a way of seeing whether the choking is simply the physical manifestation of a more deep-rooted psychological illness.

Of course prevention is better than cure. Over millions of years of evolution fish have developed a defence mechanism whereby if they are eaten by a human half their entire skeleton lodges in the throat. You can avoid this by ordering fish fingers in smart seafood restaurants.

However, don't be silly about preventive medicine. It's not very clever preventively thumping people on the back on the off-chance that they might be about to choke. First, you will project the contents of their mouth three yards across the tablecloth, and second, you will be the person who ends up choking due to the subsequent strangling effect of their hands around your neck.

The other persistent choking hazards are small objects which have some kind of strange gravitational pull towards the throat. A fail-safe means of avoiding this hazard is to wear wicketkeeper's gloves at all times. In this way you will find it virtually impossible to pick up anything small enough to get lodged in your windpipe. There's also an evens chance you'll get picked for the England eleven.

The general rule is don't put anything small in your mouth that you're likely to swallow. Unless, of course, it's food. Then you should cut up everything into pieces that would fit gaily through the eye of a large darning needle. For safety's sake, don't talk or laugh while you're eating. Sit up straight and look directly ahead. If you do this on a regular basis, the chances of your choking will be much reduced, as will your chances of having an interesting dinner companion.

How to... die

Death can be as simple as falling off a log. Which is why you should steer clear of logs. Eventually death stares us all in the face – even people who've had their faces lifted. For people with facelifts, death has to look up slightly, but you still get the same effect, i.e. death.

The best way of preparing for death is to make sure you have a good life. This doesn't mean you should live each day as if it were your last. You don't want to spend every day of your life with eighteen anxious relatives around your bed and a priest warming up in the hall.

Be suspicious of famous last words. To say something memorable before you die, you either have to say something memorable and then completely shut up until you die, or you have to say something memorable every five seconds. If you've never said anything faintly interesting in your whole life, make sure you have someone interesting at your bedside. When you feel yourself going, mumble 'Take the bins out'. They will translate this into something memorable, like 'I am blinded by visions of glory'.

Dying suddenly is quite easy, as you don't have to practise and make peace with people you don't like. Being terminally ill and knowing you're going to die sooner rather than later is trickier. One of the trickiest things is that most terminal illnesses are deeply unpleasant. Why aren't any terminal illnesses exciting and physically pleasurable? There are a few people who die of a surfeit of pleasure in a massive drugs binge. They're probably still thinking that they're on the longest and weirdest trip they've ever been on.

When you're dying you begin to realize for the first time how miraculous and passing beautiful life really is. At this stage it can be difficult to appreciate the jigsaw of Poole Harbour that someone brings you to fill in the time before death.

Death is often more difficult for the people left behind. That's because death is a dirty word in our society and people treat the bereaved as if you've tucked your skirt into your knickers – something dreadful has clearly happened, but no one can bring themselves to talk to you about it.

Wills are the last chance to interact with the living, so make sure you include a few surprises. Leave a pair of your underpants to your lawyers, or leave something really valuable that you don't actually own to someone greedy so that they can spend their life looking for it. Or endow a local bakery to bake coffee and walnut cake for your spouse in perpetuity. Just because you're dying doesn't mean you can't have a bit of fun.

COOKING AND EATING

How to... make toast

Toast is the thin white line that stands between millions of young single men and starvation. When mothers insist that their young men get three square meals a day, this is usually translated into three square slices of bread lightly browned in the toaster.

Brown toast isn't really much good because it doesn't change colour when you toast it. Brown bread already has a lot of attitude (as well as all sorts of bits from the bakery floor), and toasting it is like punishing it for being too good for you in its natural state. With white bread you feel as though you're doing it a favour toasting it. It's like two weeks in the Caribbean for it.

Some people cut off the crusts of their toast. These are people who don't understand where real pleasure lies – the sort of people who wear cycle helmets in the country and have sex in their pyjamas. The whole point of toast is that it is crusty, crunchy, crispy and crustacean.

In toasting terms, sliced bread is clearly the best thing since sliced bread. However, the good thing about cutting your own bread is that you can put huge doorsteps in the toaster, which you then have to crush down with your hand. This prevents the toast being ripped to pieces when you attempt to spread butter on it.

Making toast may look simple, but it isn't, and that's why no one else can ever make it quite the way you like it. For example, some people absolutely insist you spread the jam to the furthest corners of the toast. Others insist on jam applied in Marmite-sized quantities. Still others insist on Marmite applied in jam-sized quantities. These last don't normally have friends prepared to make toast for them.

Cold toast is a very sad affair and gives a small insight into death – something you've known and loved, that was warm and comforting, but is now cold and stiff and destined for the bin. If this thought gets you down, pop in another couple of slices and smear them with half a pound of butter and honey. If that doesn't cheer you up, then nothing will.

Toasters are one of the high points of Western civilization, and it's only a shame that you can't cook bigger meals like roast beef or country chicken pie in them. The quintessence of toast is thick white bread, well browned but not burned, hand-crushed and then soaked in salted butter with a layer of tangy marmalade on top. That's real cooking, and that is why millions of single men choose it over a lot of fancy restaurant cuisine. Unless someone else is paying.

How to... make a
good cup of tea

A good cup of tea is one you can offer your plumber with no risk that he will then link up your bathroom taps to your electricity supply. This rules out any kind of fruit or herbal tea. The only possible exception to this is if your plumber shows up and says, 'Any chance of a herbal infusion, love?' There has been no evidence of this happening so far in recorded history.

Other weirdo teas don't count either. Earl Grey tastes like someone has dropped a cigarette in dishwater and people who drink it tend to wear loose clothing and get tired easily. Similarly, steer clear of teas that sound like a developing world folk band, such as lapsang souchong. Real tea comes in bags, and that doesn't mean little raffia sacks in a delicatessen. If you can't buy your tea in boxes of 240 bags, then you're being sold a pup. Real tea is what the army refers to as Nato Standard. This is a dark brown colour with full-fat milk and two heaped sugars. Anything less and Nato would be seriously weakened.

Here's how to make it. While waiting for the kettle to boil, put one bag in the bottom of your mug. Some people boast that they can make ten cups of tea from one bag and you'll find them hanging out the used ones to

51

dry. It's people like this who are mostly responsible for Britain's economic decline.

Pour on the water and then add milk. Then get your teaspoon out and give the bag a good bashing. This is where the artistry of tea making resides. The trick is to swill the bag around until your tea is slightly weaker than desired. You then give the bag a little squeeze with your thumb to bring it up to strength. Just squeeze until your thumb burns.

Give the tea a preliminary stir to check for strength. Only add more milk as a last resort as it's impossible to add a drop from a 4-pint plastic carton. Unless you've got the reactions of Zorro, a drop from one of these beasts tends to be about half a pint.

Finally, add sugar. Two sugars is the norm for working people. Tea without sugar is an admission that what you do in life doesn't require that much effort. If someone else is making tea for you, then it's best to ask for three sugars because people who don't take sugar can't stir tea properly (generally because they haven't got enough energy).

How to... eat sweets

You can tell how serious a person is about chocolate by how much wrapping they're prepared to tolerate. Poncey Continental chocolates nestling in a sea of plastic don't have the same therapeutic impact as a 1 kg slab in easy-rip wrapping. Remember, those lines on chocolate bars are serving suggestions only. You can actually eat the whole thing and no one will be any the wiser.

Some people are given a box of chocolates at Christmas and will eat one on special occasions over the next year or so. They get as much pleasure browsing through the tin as they do eating their single hazelnut dervish. Normal people view a tin of chocolates more like a nosebag. Once it's been opened, it has to be emptied and the fiddly wrappers are the only brake on consumption.

Everyone has a favourite in a box of chocolates. You're either a nut person, a fudge person, or a cream person. To have a long-term relationship, it's advisable to make sure you're not both the same. Starting on the bottom tray before the top tray has been finished is the devil's work. Even if the last one on the top layer is a disgusting praline prepuce, you've got to choke it down before you can go for the orange cream downstairs.

With boiled sweets, you're either a cruncher or sucker. You can offer some people a boiled sweet and they'll still be sucking it when you next see them a week later. For them it's a kind of spiritual exercise to see how long they can keep a sweet alive, and they would die happy as long as they had a tiny sliver of it still on their tongue.

If you're sitting down to a packet of sweets, it's often a good idea to empty them out and then order them by flavour. If you've got more strawberries than lemons you can then start with the strawberries until you have exactly the same number of each. Then it's simply a case of eating them in turn, starting with the ones you hate first.

When you have to share sweets, you can offer them first or eat one first, depending on the exact position of the black one. Be careful you don't give your friend every single yellow one in the pack, otherwise they might think you're using them for waste disposal purposes.

Pick 'n' mix works on the basis that what you're picking looks so tiny that what you end up with will be cheap. In reality, once you've had a trowelful of everything you fancy, you end up lugging the weight equivalent of a bag of cement to the till and paying three times the price of your cinema ticket.

How to... have good table manners

If you want to make any sort of progress in today's world, you have to know how to handle two things: a golf mallet and a fish knife. This is because the only time people talk to each other is when they're eating or playing golf. With golf you can get away with continual swearing, but table manners are a sterner test.

First, you should never start eating before anyone else, does although it's worth making a quiet check on whether they actually ordered a starter. Once you get started, you'll often have more cutlery in front of you than you have in your drawer at home. The polite thing to do is to make sure that you use every single implement on every course, even if it's soup. After you've used an implement, store it in the little jug marked with the flower.

At some stage the waiter may bring a bottle of wine for your approval. The correct thing to do is to check the alcohol content. If it's lower than 15 per cent, send it straight back. Once you've checked the alcohol content, they will pour a tiny amount into your glass. This is sheer meanness on their part. You've paid for it, so insist on a full glass. You can then go ahead and taste the wine.

Just remember that spitting it out is the right thing to do, and the correct receptacle for this is the ice bucket beside the table of the romantic couple sitting next to you.

Napkin folding is one of the cornerstones of Western civilization, and staff in a good restaurant should be able to transform a damask napkin into a fully functioning stegosaurus in less time than it takes you to find the right end of an asparagus spear. Waiting staff are always happy to demonstrate this skill, so wait until they've spread it across your lap and then say you preferred it in its mating duck form. There is often some confusion between a napkin and a serviette, and getting it wrong is a clear signal that you are as common as dirt. The golden rule is that where there is an even number dining, napkins are serviettes, and vice versa.

Certain foods have for years provided a litmus test for social skills. For example, asking for two fish fingers is tantamount to slapping your host in the face. Similarly, taking a mouthful of alphabet soup without a vowel is wretchedly common. The ultimate challenge, of course, is lobster when you're given a bowl and a pair of nut-crackers. It takes years of practice to find the lobster's nuts and then transfer them to the bowl, but socially it pays huge dividends.

How to... use a fridge

Before fridges were invented, people had to eat things fast before they went off. But, as there weren't any 'best before' dates, the only rule was that you had to eat something before something airborne or bacteriological started eating it for you.

There are certain items that live permanently in the fridge for the whole lifetime of the fridge. Among these are a half-used tube of tomato purée, a bottle of lemon juice and an old boiled egg. There's also a bottle of ointment, with a sticky lid, for a medical purpose so private no one wants to mention it.

Some people can go to the fridge and rustle up a three-course meal made entirely from leftovers. The question is, if they're such great cooks, why do they have so many leftovers?

The fridge is the natural home for milk. In fact, if there's only one thing in the fridge, it's going to be milk. That's because a house without milk is a house incapable of making tea and therefore to all intents and purposes a dead house. That's why the top priority when you get back from holiday is to get some milk in the fridge.

Most fridges have little drawers for the salad things to go in. This is because tomatoes, etc. don't like being seen in the raw and demand a little bit of privacy. It's also a great way of forgetting all about your salad until it's time to throw it away.

In many houses the fridge serves as the communal noticeboard. Messages on the door in magnetic letters are always slightly contrived as you never have enough vowels to say exactly what you want. Messages on the inside are more along the lines of 'I have measured the exact angle of this slice of chocolate cake. Shaving bits off will result in your disembowelment.'

Philosophers have often speculated whether the fridge light is still on when the door is closed. In return, fridges often speculate whether philosophers still talk rubbish when they take their corduroy jackets off.

For a piece of food, being put in the freezer compartment is like being a CV that's put on file. Technically, you could be used, but in reality you've been forgotten. Of course, some foods live in the freezer. Ice cream can survive for years in there, or up to seven hours if there's a woman in the house. Defrosting the freezer should be done every six months but in reality happens as often as the passing of an ice age. If you find a woolly mammoth in your drip tray, you've probably left it too long.

How to... eat biscuits

In northern cultures the dunking of the biscuit represents the sun disappearing below the horizon at the end of the day. An alternative explanation is that it's a way of making your biscuits slightly wetter and more tasty.

Dunking biscuits is like Russian roulette except without the gun, bullets or anything Russian. Most people opt for the safety dunk, where you just dip a little bit of the biscuit in and then suck off the soggy bit. More dangerous is the slam dunk, where you put the entire biscuit in up to your fingertips and then whip it out at the last moment. There is a very real risk that you'll end up with the entire body of your biscuit lying cementified on the bottom of your mug. This gives an opportunity for those who don't dunk to feel fantastically superior. Non-dunkers say they enjoy the contrast between warm and wet and dry and hard. Perverts.

Expert dunkers can dunk a custard cream so that the biscuit parts can be sucked off leaving only the custard bit in the middle. Similarly, people often nibble all the chocolate off a chocolate biscuit, leaving its little naked body shivering and defenceless. But if they like chocolate that much why don't they just buy a bar of chocolate?

For some women a packet of biscuits is a sacrifice on the altar of comfort, with many associated rituals. For example, a biscuit is a tempting thing, but once it is eaten its power to tempt is destroyed. Therefore, the more biscuits you eat, the more the temptation is reduced. This is an important principle in dieting. Similarly, once a third of the packet has been eaten, the remainder of the packet becomes administratively awkward and has to be finished for the sake of tidiness.

Biscuit crumbs are an occupational hazard for biscuit eaters. That's why many people employ the bite and suck method, whereby the desired portion of the biscuit is bitten off while a vigorous sucking action collects the crumbs. Of course, this is often a complete waste of time as the bit you're still holding usually disintegrates at this point. The only realistic solution is to put the whole biscuit straight in your mouth (go easy if it's a Wagon Wheel).

For some reason, biscuits from a packet always taste a lot better than biscuits from a tin. That's because the joy of eating biscuits is that they are all exactly the same. It's not like having a meal where you have to have bits of this and bits of the other. You choose which biscuit you want, and then you know it's going to be ginger nuts all the way down.

How to... cook something really impressive

If you want to cook something really impressive, really fresh ingredients are vital and the fresher they are the better. Ideally, you should be ripping lettuces out of their beds before dawn, and eggs shouldn't be allowed to hit the ground beneath the hen.

The next vital step is to get a completely new kitchen. It should be a combination of stainless-steel surfaces you could perform an appendectomy on and heavy wooden units to give the air of a country kitchen. Then hang pots, pans and utensils from the ceiling of your kitchen. This has the advantage of getting them out your way; the disadvantage is that they are now in the last place on earth you'd look for them.

Now put on an apron. It doesn't matter what the pattern is as long as the strings go round you twice and tie up at the front. Remember, the funnier your apron is, the less chance your pavlova will be successful.

Then arrange all your ingredients on a worktop and make sure none of the colours clash. Finely slice your ingredients with a knife so sharp you don't notice two of your fingers missing. Before you use them, look once more at your ingredients, and resign yourself to the fact that they'll never look that good again.

Pour yourself a drink in the full knowledge that when things get desperate on the stove you're likely to tip half your drink in for added 'inspiration' – it's therefore not a good idea to be sipping crème de menthe or banana daiquiri.

Make sure you have a complete set of herb and spices. There are approximately 465 herbs and spices, and the one you haven't got is the one you need – don't panic if this happens, just tip your drink in.

Set aside an hour to sculpt a large carrot – fifty-five minutes for butchering a bag of carrots and five minutes to realize that the ones in oriental restaurants are mass-produced by commercial laser-cutters.

Then cook very quickly or very slowly. Flash frying is very impressive, as is cooking something for a week in a haybox. Don't ever admit to an hour at gas mark 6 unless shepherd's pie is your idea of sophistication.

Heat your plates up until they're red hot. This always gives the impression that you are a restaurant-standard caterer. Don't spoil this impression by covering the plates with steel helmets and whipping them off at the last moment. Unless you've prepared baked Viking's head, what's under the helmet is invariably a disappointment.

How to... use a knife and fork

What separates mankind from the animals is our use of tools. Although you wouldn't have guessed it from the way some people use their knives and forks.

There's currently a lot of debate as to which way up you should hold your fork. The golden rule is that if you're using it to spoon things you should be using a spoon and if you're using it to cut things you should be using a knife. Forks have prongs so you can prong things.

Forks can be used as a holding device while you cut things or as a rake to gather far-flung bits of dinner into the central killing zone. Forks are also the main form of transport to your mouth. There are European regulations governing the amount of food you are allowed to transport to your mouth on a fork. For good manners, you should only carry as much food as you can put in your mouth at one time and still talk freely.

Peas are the big test for forks. Some people choose to spear them individually. This is the Moby Dick option because like the hunt for Moby Dick, it's likely to prove largely unsuccessful and drive you to madness. Or you can herd your peas into your mashed potato and scoop them both up (this is how mushy peas evolved). One day, genetic modification will bring us the square pea and all these troubles will be over.

The knife serves as a surrogate pair of teeth. In the wild you would rip off what you needed with your teeth. Nowadays, this is still possible with sandwiches but not such a good idea with a plate of roast pork. You might be able to rip off a piece of crackling, but you'll end up with your forehead in the red cabbage.

Just because it's a knife doesn't mean you have to hold it as if you were about to stab someone. You have to hold the knife as if it were a pen (unless you're in the habit of stabbing people with pens). For those interested in advanced etiquette, it's the height of bad manners to stab someone with a fish knife unless they are a Pisces.

Knives are also good for spreading things. It's almost like turning swords into ploughshares. One moment you're cutting things to pieces, the next you're spreading things around in a sharing fashion. Finally, beware of the fishcake: experts are still undecided whether it should be approached with a fish knife or cake fork. If in doubt, don't approach it and edge quietly backwards until you are out of danger.

GUY BROWNING

How to... eat ice cream

Women have a much deeper and more intense relationship with ice cream than they do with men. That's because with ice cream you get a lot more variety and a greater sense of physical satisfaction.

Deciding on what ice cream to have is one of the most complex decisions known to woman. Generally, you're either a fruity woman or a dark chocolate/caramel/coffee woman. Vanilla women don't really exist and you're probably dealing with a man in drag. Women will try any new flavour of ice cream once. There is something mystical about the state of ice creaminess, and anything that has been elevated to that condition, be it sausages, carrots or petroleum jelly, deserves respect.

The quantity of ice cream to eat is an easier decision: however much there is available is one portion. Cute little individual tubs are like tester paint pots: they give you a clue as to what effect you'll get once you crack open the proper industrial-size tub. Similarly, when you're having a cone, one scoop is a sure sign you don't really like ice cream. Those cones have been tested up to a maximum of five scoops, and three scoops is a sensible minimum for a growing woman.

One way of making sure you're not at the mercy of ice cream shops is to have a freezer at home that has a bigger and better selection than the shops and 24-hour opening. Just remember to get your favourite ice cream out ten minutes before you need it. There's nothing worse than sitting down to your favourite soap and then having to wrestle with a power saw and blowtorch to get a decent scoop from the tub.

A really difficult decision is whether to share ice cream. This decision is often made for you by the flavour. Obviously, you can hand out vanilla left, right and centre; but if it's a holy grail flavour that you can only find in one specialist supermarket in Truro, then you should eat the entire tub under a thick towel with the phone off the hook. In the worst-case scenario, when a so-called friend asks for a spoon, offer her a teaspoon and give yourself a reasonable headstart with a ladle.

Ice cream is a comfort food; when you're in front of the TV with a bowl of Belgian white chocolate ice cream, you've got everything required for complete happiness. Oh, and a man to get the refills.

How to... diet

The purpose of dieting is to lose weight so that you will become more attractive to the opposite sex, who will then invite you out to expensive restaurants where you can eat like a hog. Lots of people overeat because in our abundant society food is never more than a thirty-second walk away. Therefore a good way to reduce your calorie consumption is to locate yourself in a wilderness where there is no food – a train, for example.

There are as many different diets as there are excuses to eat biscuits. There's the F-plan, C-plan and so on. The most effective is the X-plan diet: you can eat anything you like so long as it has an 'x' in it. One useful tip is to keep a list of everything you eat. This is especially good for big eaters as compiling a massive long list can actually cut down the time you spend eating. Finally, when you've finished the list, eat it. That's your meal for the day.

Crash diets are where you can lose a stone in a week. This is otherwise known as amputation. For the really serious, you can have your jaws wired together, which means you have to exist on energy drinks and high carbohydrate suppositories. But remember, having your jaws wired together might also have a detrimental impact on your career in telesales.

You will eat less if you learn to chew slowly and savour your food. If you chew each mouthful 380 times you will cut down your food intake dramatically as it will take you a week to get through a cheese sandwich. Avoid using this technique during important business lunches.

A great idea to make you think twice about eating is to consider where you're going to store the food you eat when your stomach is already full. For example, imagine that huge slice of chocolate cake being stored on your thighs. Go easy with this visualization technique because you might start to associate your thighs with chocolate cake and wake up to find yourself munching away at your leg.

You can also try a treats and rewards system, where you punish yourself with a stick of celery for lunch and reward yourself with a Mars bar for afters. Really fat people who eat nothing but junk food are using the same system: they reward themselves with tasty junk food for their whole life and punish themselves by an early death.

Finally, if you're binge eating, the real question you should be asking yourself is not what you're eating, but what's eating you. If you look down and you're in fact being eaten by a coypu, there's your answer.

FASHION AND GROOMING

How to... be beautiful

Beauty may only be skin-deep, but let's face it, no one's in a hurry to go out with a good-looking pancreas. In general, beauty is in the eye of the beholder, especially when alcohol goes into the mouth of the beholder at roughly the same time.

Facelifts are a popular way of keeping your looks for longer, although you don't often hear younger people saying to each other, 'I love your high face.' You can now get Botox injections which freeze your face in position. Traditionally, you could get the same kind of frozen face every time Uncle Ralph told one of his jokes. The cheapest and most effective facelift is the smile. The quickest way to smile is when someone says that you're looking beautiful. Which is why most people continue to look grumpy.

Women make up their faces to appear more attractive, while men make up things about themselves to appear more attractive. With women, the more make-up they use, the less attractive they think they are. Men don't like a lot of make-up on women, partly because it's like kissing a recently laid pavement and partly because they don't want to wait the hour and a half it takes women to put it on.

Doing beautiful things can make you appear very beautiful. That's why public sector workers are generally accepted to be better-looking than those in the private sector. The only things that stop most people being beautiful are superficialities like hair, nose, eyes, skin, legs, body, clothing and personality. Seeing past these requires the miracle X-ray specs of love. The really amazing thing is that someone out there somewhere will find you beautiful even though you've always thought of yourself as being a bit of a Mr Potato Head. You may have to wait for incredibly sympathetic lighting conditions for that to happen, but it will.

Interestingly, most people, even though they know they're two Humbrol pots short of being an oil painting, secretly think they have one or two beautiful bits. For example, the old troll in the dry cleaners may quietly believe she has very attractive feet. When her Prince Charming eventually comes in with his soiled doublet for cleaning, her beautiful feet will be the first thing he notices.

Some people start ugly but become beautiful, like the ugly duckling. But if you are young and ugly you should brace yourself for the fact that most ugly ducklings grow up to be ugly ducks. On the other hand, swans make a nasty hiss while ducks make a lovely quack. There's got to be a moral there somewhere.

How to... wear shorts

The British climate is designed on the principle that grey is the new blue. Oddly, we have given the world an item of clothing spectacularly unsuited to this climate – the pair of shorts. In our wisdom we have developed an item of clothing that directs water down our legs, wind onto our kidneys, and frost onto our extremities.

There was a time not so long ago when the first time a British male was allowed into long trousers was when he left school for the army. Even then some regiments prided themselves on wearing shorts, on the basis that if someone laughs at your trousers you'll be more inclined to kill them (hence the fierce fighting reputation of the Scots regiments, who have to suffer an almost continuous barrage of raucous laughter at their chosen battledress).

Traditionally, shorts came down to just above the knee, revealing a kneecap indistinguishable from a good-size Desiree potato. A gartered sock then led down from the knee to the stout ankle boot at the bottom. However, withdrawal from empire has coincided with an ever-increasing shortness of shorts and wanton exposure of leg.

The human body has not been designed to look good in shorts, and therefore if you want to get away with it you must stick to the golden rule of shorts wearing: shorts mustn't be shorter than your underpants or longer than long trousers. Your buttock cleavage should not be visible above the waistline nor should your buttocks hang out from the bottom of your shorts (especially if you're wearing Bermuda shorts). If your buttocks are visible both above and below your shorts you've probably been sold a thong.

Cut-offs are not fashionable, and definitely won't be if the bit you cut off wasn't fashionable in the first place. Unless you're a country-and-western singer with a name like Petty Cash, don't wear sawn-off jeans with frayed edges. Similarly, never wear a belt with your shorts unless you are a Venture Scout or an Ivy League American or don't mind registering zero on the hip-factor scale.

There is currently a fashion among youths to wear incredibly long shorts with big pockets for carrying surfboards around in. Some of these shorts are so cool and so long that they go through a barrier of cool and become nerdy long trousers that aren't quite long enough. Strangely, this barrier is only crossed if over-thirties put on a pair.

How to... wear a hat

Fifty years ago, if you went out without a hat you were obviously a little bit eccentric. Today, if you go out with a hat you're obviously as mad as a hatter. The reason for this is that shampoo manufacturers have better marketing departments than milliners. No one in a million years is going to try and sell you a beret by persuading you that 'You're worth it.' In fact, if you get into a bit of an ugly situation in a pub and you happen to be wearing a beret, it's more than likely that someone is going to say, 'Leave him, Kev, he's not worth it.'

That's because wearing a beret is like stepping into a social black hole. There may be life on the other side, but no one can be quite sure what. A beret is a soft hat and as such is at the far end of the spectrum from the hard hat, which most men would give their right arm to wear. The hard hat is the equivalent of having a flashing orange light on your head; it means 'I am occupied in dangerous, manly work; you could get hurt, so stand clear.' Men often leave a hard hat on the parcel shelf at the back of their car to warn people not to park too close as they may need to get a power tool from the boot at any time.

The only acceptable hats for men to wear on the street are the woolly rapper-style hats with names across the front. Never ask your mother to make you one of these hats because, however strict your instructions are, you will get a hat with a bobble on the top, and there hasn't been a successful rapper yet who wears a bobble hat. Grandmothers will knit you hats whether you ask for one or not as they were brought up to believe that no skin should show between your socks, pants and hat. Brace yourself for an all-in-one long-john balaclava that keeps your head warm and the draught off your kidneys.

Women only wear hats on high days and bad hair days. For some reason, women have to buy hats for weddings, generally in bright colours with big rims. At a wedding, if you sit at the back of a church full of hatted women, it looks spookily like a parking lot for the Jetsons' spacecraft. This is a very subtle ploy to make everyone look silly except the bride (and the groom in the beret).

How to... wear glasses

The world can be divided into two kinds of people: those who wear glasses, and those who think they don't need glasses. You can spot the first group because they're wearing glasses. The second group are also easy to spot because they walk past you in corridors, park on your front lawn, and screw their eyes up when you ask them if they can see the double-decker bus in front of them.

Once you decide to get glasses you need to choose which type. Generally, there are two kinds of glasses you'll need: there are the ones you need for reading, and there are the ones you need to find the ones you need for reading.

Avoid bifocals: these have a nasty line halfway up the lens that gives the impression that your head is half-full. Bifocals mean you can't read anything higher than your chest or see anything coming lower than your chest. They're obviously a nightmare for short people reading timetables at bus stops and looking for the bus coming up the hill. Varifocals mean you can focus clearly on anything so long as you keep your head permanently in motion.

You can repair your own glasses. If the bridge breaks, simply wind a yard of sellotape around it. Similarly, if one of the ear struts goes you can keep your glasses on your head with a thick piece of elastic. Remember, personality is more important than looks.

People with limited personality can buy cool, trendy frames. The rule is the straighter the frame, the cooler you are; and the rounder, the squarer. Red-framed glasses are not cool, have never been cool, and never will be cool. Red glasses suit nobody. Everyone in the world knows this apart from a very small number of people who buy glasses with red frames.

There's an old saying that men don't make passes at women with glasses. That's generally because women with glasses can see what's on offer and make themselves scarce. Some older women wear glasses that hang from gold chains around their necks. This is code for 'I am open to suggestions of sexual practices involving chains and bondage.' Ask them about it next time you're in the library.

Buying glasses is a slightly bizarre experience in that you go into an optician with lots of lovely frames, you pick a pair you like, slip them on, go to the mirror and realize you can't see a bloody thing. Once you get glasses you actually look rather clever, especially if before you got them you spent a lot of time walking face-first into lamp-posts and off cliffs.

How to... have big ears

Having big ears is one of the oddest peculiarities to have because no one quite knows what it means. For example, if you're a man with big ears, women don't titter in the street, wink knowingly and say look at the size of his ears. Or they might do, but that's the end of the conversation.

Women don't really have a big ear problem as they can grow their hair over them. All you have to remember is to go for big hair all over. Simply growing hair over the affected area will make you look as though you're wearing earmuffs.

Some lobally challenged people refer laughingly to their big ears as love handles. This is not meant to be taken literally and if, during carnal transport, they are handled excessively, the big-eared may well feel that their lover is fantasizing about making love to a hobbit.

There comes a time in the life of every big-eared football player when his friends will decide he resembles the FA Cup. This is OK as far as it goes, but when the whole team decides to tie coloured ribbons on the handles and parade 'the Cup' around the pitch, then the amusement factor tends to tail off, especially for the person between the ears.

Some famous people have been known to glue their ears down in order to make themselves seem more streamlined. The trick here is to make sure the glue is strong enough. There's nothing worse than making a big social entrance with your nicely flush ears only to have one suddenly break free and fly open like a taxi door.

Big ear owners, like Battle of Britain pilots, are constantly aware of the position of the sun. When the sun gets behind your ears it gaily shines straight through them, making you look as though you've got a couple of Chinese lanterns attached to your head. If a group of people are laughing unexpectedly at you and you know you've got a big pair of rubbery flappers, check the sun.

When night falls, the trials of the big-eared are far from over. Turning over on your pillow requires as much attention to the positioning of the ears as a pilot would give to the positioning of the undercarriage on landing. If you accidentally fold an ear over and spend the night with the weight of your head on it, not only will it stick out in the morning but there's a very good chance that it will be pointing forward. And that's a distinction you don't need on a crowded bus. Especially if it's on its way to the Cup Final.

How to... appear taller

It is a fact that in Britain there are almost no men at all who measure either 5' 10" or 5' 11". Instead, there is a statistically baffling concentration of men at the 6' 00" mark. That's because ever since mankind has walked erect he has worried about the measurable extent of his erection.

One easy way of appearing taller is to wear high heels. This is acceptable for women but not for men, unless they want to be mistaken for a woman. Instead, men have to wear their high heels inside their shoes. You can buy shoes that are built up to give you an extra foot without anyone noticing (except when you go swimming and disappear in the shallow end).

Another option is to hang around with short people and look down on them – this is not so easy, as the last thing really short people want is to be lorded over by averagely short people. Short people in general are popular because they make other people feel taller – how else do you explain the attraction of Napoleon who made his entire army feel bigger and butcher than they really were?

Standing tall is clearly important. Put your feet together, lock knees and reach for the sky with the top of your head. This will give you an extra inch or so but will make you liable to be blown over in high winds, and will also give the impression that you have industrial-strength piles.

After a good night's sleep most people gain about half an inch in height, so try and schedule important meetings for immediately after you've woken up.

It's amazing how many people you know to be vertically challenged appear to be much, much taller in photographs. That's because they have developed the ability to find, in a split second, something to stand on – such as a kerb, step, ledge, box, or the missing person in the photo.

It may sound trite, but if you want to appear taller you need to think taller – take up high jumping and basketball; talk down to tall people by throwing your head right back as if you were going to sneeze; duck as you go through doorways, even if you're 5' 4" and have about three feet of clearance.

Finally, refuse to acknowledge that other people are taller than you. Simply talk to the bit of their anatomy which is at your eye level and pretty soon they'll be crouching and bending down like someone trying to look through a letterbox.

How to... be bald

Women rate baldness somewhere below webbed feet in what they are looking for in a man. Men know this, especially bald men. Therefore bald men are divided into those who worry about it greatly and those who don't really pay much attention to what women want, on the basis that women never really know what they want anyway. If you're going bald, the trick is not to worry about it. Worry leads to anxiety which leads to stress which leads to hair loss. In fact, if you're really happy about losing your hair, the chances are that it will stay put just to spite you.

Hair transplants are where a small portion of hair-growing skin is taken from one part of your body and relaid on your head in the same way that you turf a lawn. You may get new hair in this way, but your hair-style will look suspiciously like an armpit and your head may give off a nasty locker-room tang. Sidewinding is an alternative approach. Sidewinders have an amazing capacity for self-delusion in that they look in the mirror and see a man with a full head of hair. Everyone else sees a baldy with a long strand of hair coiled on top of his head.

Once you've lost the final strands and you still can't face the world without hair, the wig is your only option. Wigs come in two styles, laughable and ridiculous, and two colours, jet black and bleached blond. If you're over sixty and you wear a jet-black wig, people aren't going to wonder why you haven't got grey hair, they're going to wonder why you don't have any friends kind enough to tell you that you look like an extra from the *Return of the Living Dead*.

Most men lose their hair very gradually – so if you keep your hairstyle the same, people won't notice it going (except at school reunions). Any drastic change in hairstyle, such as switching from brushing back to brushing forward, instantly puts everyone on chrome-dome alert. Some men discover a little circle of skin blossoming on top of their head. You'll know who these men are because they never allow you to get into a position where you can look down on them.

The difference between a receding hairline and genuine slapheadedness is the difference between recession and depression. You know you've finally left hair behind when you trust your partner to cut your hair because there really isn't much damage they can do. Of course, the one consolation about being bald is that you are much, much better in bed than your hirsute friends. Sadly, you're unlikely to get much chance to prove it.

How to... polish shoes

In the old days, about a third of the population was engaged in polishing something or other – from silver to horse brasses to their front doorsteps. Nowadays we only polish our shoes – and we only polish them before an interview because we all know that what employers want these days more than anything else is shiny shoes. Therefore, until genetic modification of cows give us the self-polishing shoe, we will have to keep the old shoe-shining arts alive.

To polish shoes you first have to remove the larger debris, like twigs, chewing gum, mud, sweet wrappers, tar, rotting fruit, grass cuttings, horse dung, roadkill, etc. Put these to one side for making a tasty stock later.

Next apply the polish. It's worth getting an expensive wax polish because cheaper ones are usually made of the same stuff that you've just scraped off. (Remember to match up the colour of your polish with the colour of your shoe. However hard you shine, black polish won't come up red.)

For maximum involvement with your shoe, apply the polish with your fingers and a damp cloth. This heats and lubricates the polish at the same time, allowing the wax to sink into the shoe. (Now you know why businessmen wear black socks.)

Spit and polish go together like love and marriage, but don't spit on your shoe (or your spouse) during any kind of heavy cold. Also, unless you can hit a spittoon at forty paces, spit on a cloth first rather than attempting to hit your shoe. The last thing you want after you've got your shoes perfect for an interview is to slip your foot into a half an inch of phlegm.

Shining requires a huge amount of elbow grease. Basically, you rub like a loony and put more energy into one minute's polishing than into a month of housework (a year's housework for a man). Then you begin to understand why polishing two pairs of shoes is the aerobic equivalent of running a half-marathon on your hands, and why basic training in the army is 10 per cent running and 90 per cent polishing.

Finally, stand back and admire the way you've polished your shoes, 90 per cent of your exposed flesh, and all local soft furnishings, and at the same time virtually guaranteed yourself a job offer in a high-tech industry.

How to... manage socks

Socks lead lives strangely similar to our own. They know they should be in pairs but they can't help detaching themselves. Like us, they relish their freedom for a brief moment and then find themselves down the back of the radiator of life.

In the old days, if your sock had a hole in it you darned it. Old socks used to be darned so many times that there would be none of the original sock left, only darn. All the original sock would then be on someone else's foot. For a time it used to be possible to buy indestructible socks made from some kind of nylon–polystyrene mix. Over a period of time they actually caused holes in your shoes and your feet.

One of the difficulties of living with someone is when you have different but similar socks. One partner will absolutely insist that socks be reunited with their soulmates. The other will put any old socks together as long as they're roughly similar. Then, halfway through a key interview, you discover that Miffy is peeking out of the bottom of your trouser leg.

Everyone has, somewhere in their possession, a really

thick pair of woollen socks for use in rambling-type situations. Funnily enough, the only colour these socks don't come in is black, because no one rambles to the office.

Socks need to be changed regularly as walking around all day can be hot work. The rule for men is that socks should be changed half as often as pants and twice as often as trousers. In reality, men often tend to leave socks until they walk across the room and throw themselves into the laundry basket.

You can tell a lot about a person by their sock drawer. If they have a sock drawer in the first place, they're likely to pay regularly into a pension. Inside the drawer, if the socks are laid out like a pack of Cumberland sausages and used in strict rotation, their owner is unlikely to be a wild thing in bed.

Beware men who wear sawn-off tights as socks. They will generally try to sell you something or get you into bed or sell you a bed. Also beware of men who don't own any socks. They invariably have the world's ugliest fifteen-jointed toes.

Although socks are technically underwear, they are in no way sexy. It's absolutely vital when undressing in front of your lover, not to find yourself in the dreaded socks–pants combo. For some reason this is an absolute turn-off. Which is why lingerie departments don't have any bra–knickers–socks sets.

How to... be fashionable

Being fashionable is the in-thing at the moment. In fashion, new is the new new. Even if it's the turn of old to be the new new, it's the new old that's the new new and not the old old, because old is the old old and is never going to be the new anything ever again.

All fashion is cool. It's cool even though much of it has ordinary people rolling in the aisles laughing themselves sick. That's why ordinary people aren't allowed into fashion shows, because they'd clog up the aisles and cause a fire hazard. Fashionistas have the equivalent of the Official Secrets Act, whereby anybody in the industry can say anything they like about fashion so long as they take it seriously.

The last genuinely original fashion idea was in the spring collection of 1974. Nevertheless, colours, lengths, cloths and styles still have to change every season. To make sure everything changes at once in the right direction, all fashion ultimately stems from a small office in the European Commission in Brussels overseen by a hypersensitive bureaucrat.

The models who model fashion don't look like normal

people. That's because if you're wearing odd clothes it helps to look slightly odd yourself. Remember, the cooler the fashion, the odder the models. Normal people look silly in high fashion in the same way that models look silly in low fashion. On the catwalk, models are trained to walk in a certain way. Were they to walk in a normal manner, people might think they were just nipping out to the loo. Instead, they walk in a way which guarantees people look at them, if only to wonder what's wrong with their walk. No one knows why it's called a catwalk; it just seemed to work better than dogwalk.

However unfashionable you consider yourself to be, it's inevitable that once every twenty years your entire wardrobe will suddenly be in vogue. Sadly, just at the point where you could be cutting a swathe through fashionable society, your clothes are borrowed by teenage relatives. Sometimes young people see through the sham of the fashion industry and develop their very own street style. This is exceptionally fashionable and keeps the industry alive for years afterwards.

Catwalk fashion ends up in the high street, where it is adjusted to fit normal people. It's galling to know that when you emerge from your cubicle with your hot new miniskirt on, some nine-foot model is stepping out in Milan in an ankle-length tweed skirt. Just remember, you were wearing long skirts ten years ago and it's taken her a long time to catch up.

SLEEPING AND WAKING

How to... be tired

Research has shown that a third of one's life is spent asleep. Another third is spent feeling like it would be nice to go back to bed. The final third is spent hoping that it will soon be time to go to bed.

Feeling tired is like being up and about but still having your brain under the duvet. People who do the least get the most tired. Teenagers often have to go back to bed to cope with the exhaustion brought on by the trauma of getting up. When you're really tired, even the thought of doing something is exhausting. In fact, doing something is generally less tiring than thinking about doing something.

Smiling is supposed to be good for you because it exercises many of the facial muscles. On the other hand, trying to keep your eyes open when you're exhausted uses every single one of the facial muscles, which is why it's impossible to smile at the same time. No surprise then that the first casualty of tiredness is charm. There's no such thing as an insomniac charmer. As you get more and more tired, you can't say anything charming, then you can't say anything interesting, then anything nice, followed by anything intelligible, and finally anything at all because if you moved your mouth your eyes would close.

There is a phrase which says that when you're tired of London you're tired of life. This explains why people on the Underground generally look suicidal. There's another phrase, 'Tired of Swindon, get a life', but that's slightly different.

They also say 'early to bed, early to rise, makes you healthy, wealthy and wise' – hence the national glut of rich philosopher-milkmen. A better phrase would be the complete opposite: 'late to bed, late to rise, makes you unhealthy, poor and stupid'. It won't be long before beds carry a government health warning – Lying in Kills'.

A nasty condition some people suffer from is when you get too tired to sleep. This is where the whole business of putting your head on the pillow and falling asleep is just too much effort to go through with. Equally nasty is feeling tired when you get up in the morning. This is like feeling dirty when you get out of the shower: you feel well and truly cheated.

Some people can catnap for ten minutes and then carry on as fresh as a daisy. For most normal people, having a nap is like a tiredness enhancer. You get fleeting pleasure from falling asleep, but then you wake up three hours later with a hangover, cramp, dry mouth, dead leg, gummy eye, and your important meeting sitting quietly in your office wondering if you're dead.

How to... go to sleep

Sleep is like the M25 in that having it is vital and everyone can't wait to get off. The trouble is, the harder you try, the less likely you are to get to sleep. The trick is to try really hard at whatever it is you do during the day. This has the double benefit of tiring you out and lessening whatever you generally worry about.

The skills and techniques used to get toddlers to sleep should also be applied to adults; rule number one is not to get yourself too excited before bedtime. So if you want to drop off quickly, don't do anything that'll excite you beforehand – like sex, for example. Driving has a miraculously soporific effect on toddlers. Similarly, visualizing your drive to work is a very good way of dropping off, as it's generally something you can do in your sleep and your mind won't bother to stay awake for it. However, if you've driven right past your office, onto the motorway, you're nearly at the Channel ports, and you've been visualizing driving for three hours non-stop, you should perhaps try a different technique.

Counting sheep is the traditional way of getting off to sleep. It's best to imagine young lambs skipping over low hedges, rather than tired old ewes with messy arses failing to get over stone walls and having to be brutally put down.

Worrying about things often keeps people awake. If you're churning things over in your mind, imagine all the images are like a television – then make the TV black and white, then make it a tiny picture, and then turn it off. This works well, especially if you also turn off the widescreen TV at the foot of your bed.

Having a warm milky drink is also an excellent way of relaxing, unless you're in a pub where ordering one is likely to cause upset all round. Don't overdo it on the evening milk drink – if you drink too much, halfway through the night you'll need milking.

Nightwear can also be an aid to sleeping. Make sure your nightwear is thick, cosy and of an extremely modest cut. This gives your body a very clear message that you definitely won't be going out or doing anything exciting in bed so you might as well go to sleep.

Sleeping pills are dangerous as they're a sure sign that you're having troubles with your days rather than your nights. Go for a long drive, throw them away, and then count sheep on your way back.

How to... keep warm in bed

There are basically two ways of keeping warm in bed. The first route is to generate heat through volcanic passion. This is great for two minutes and then you've still got the rest of the night to shiver through. It's also pretty dangerous, as getting all hot and then getting cold can give you a nasty chill.

Far better is to wear brushed-cotton pyjamas thick enough to stop armour-piercing shells. Women love men's traditional snuggly pyjamas – so much so that you generally find women inside men's traditional snuggly pyjamas. Women's full-length woolly nighties are no good for keeping warm as basically they're a tent with no groundsheet. There's also the additional hazard that you only have to turn over twice in them to be twisted tighter than a Bavarian plait.

The reason why beds get cold in the first place is that women put their feet in them. Scientific research has proved that women's feet generate more cold than the average domestic fridge-freezer. Women's feet work on the reverse principle to hot-water bottles: they're as warm as toast all day but cold, rubbery and totally unappealing during the night.

To combat this, women have evolved two techniques for keeping warm in bed. The first is that they have heat-seeking feet which migrate towards the nearest source of heat, often a man on the other side of the bed. A standard woman's foot can drain the entire body heat from an adult male in half the time it takes to fill up with a tank of unleaded. The second technique women use is duvet-winching, by which the woman turns over and pulls the duvet with her, and then keeps turning over until she is rolled up in five layers of duvet.

To keep from dying of hypothermia, men have in turn developed a range of bedroom callisthenics to generate warmth: flapping the duvet, tugging the duvet, straightening the duvet, pulling duvet down to cover feet, pulling duvet up to cover shoulders, pulling duvet off to air bed, and, finally, going to sleep in the spare room.

Beware of a woman who asks to 'spoon'. This is a deadly combination of foot-sapping and duvet-winching and can leave a man exposed to the elements within seconds. For men, that's when you need your thick pyjamas – which, of course, the woman is wearing. The only way to get them back is to go back to route one: the two minutes of volcanic passion.

How to... dream

Dreams are like low-budget British films in that they're generally badly plotted, packed with gratuitous sex and violence, and very sloppily edited. Plus, on average, one person sees them.

Dreams give you a good indication of what your mind would get up to if it weren't encumbered by your body. Which is why it's a bit disappointing that your mind is obsessed with bodily functions of one sort or another.

Freud had a lot to say about dreams. Everything wider than it is long is supposed to represent female bits, while anything longer than it is wide represents male bits. But remember that Freud used to offer his patients cheese last thing at night.

Dreams are supposed to happen during periods of rapid eye movement. In fact, the reverse is true. Once your dream gets going, your eyeballs have to work overtime to keep up with the action.

People turn up in dreams that you wouldn't want turning up on your doorstep. If you then bump into them, don't tell them they were in your dream as people always take this to mean that they were draped naked over a rug in a come-hither thong. Instead, tell them that your dream dictionary says they represent dead wood.

There are lots of standard dreams with standard interpretations. For example, all your teeth falling out means suppressed desire for your dentist. Trains rushing in and out of tunnels mean your packed sex life is just a sublimation of your secret desire to spot trains. Running naked down the street is a tricky one, especially if it involves neighbours screaming. There's a very good chance you'll wake up in a police cell with a monstrous hangover.

One of the most shameful things about being an intellectual, and one which they're not likely to admit to, is the fact that the deeper you think the more likely you are to dream in cartoons. Some of the great philosophers have been driven to the point of madness by night after night filled with Daffy Duck.

Your dream life seems more interesting than your everyday life, but it isn't really. If you took everything you did and thought in an average day and compressed it into one thirty-second blip, it would also seem pretty bizarre. Remember that your dreams are interesting to nobody but yourself. What's fascinating to you is a lot of deranged rubbish to everyone else. However, what you can do is to write your dreams down in a normal diary as if that's what you did that day and it'll confuse the hell out of your biographers.

How to... get up

Waking up in the morning is like a little birth: sometimes it's very quick and easy, and sometimes it takes many false alarms, a lot of pushing and hours of labour.

There is a very small group of people who love those quiet, peaceful moments just before the dawn. No one really knows who these people are because the rest of us are all fast asleep. A clue as to who they are comes later in the day when, just after half past seven in the evening, they say goodnight.

Some lucky people have a body clock that wakes them up precisely on time; they then feel fresh as a daisy and spring out of bed. It's great if your partner is like this when they bring you tea; it's not so good when they pull the whole duvet off and say anything which includes the phrase 'Rise and shine'.

People who have difficulty getting up have devised all sorts of foolproof ways of getting themselves out of bed. Alarm clocks which would wake the dead are great, especially if you place them out of arm's reach. However, when these go off they give you such a profound shock you have to go back to bed for an hour to get over the trauma.

Lots of people have radio-alarms which wake you up to a tiny snatch of music before you hit the snooze button. You'll know what that tiny snatch was when you're on the train an hour later singing 'A Little Bit of Monica' to yourself.

Once out of bed, there are two approaches to the day. The first is getting washed, dressed and out of the door in fifteen minutes. The second is to have a leisurely bath, choose what you're going to wear, make a cup of tea and watch a bit of breakfast TV. The bizarre thing about the second approach is that you need to get up nearly two hours earlier to allow yourself time to be leisurely.

Of course, it all boils down to whether you're a morning person or a night person. Morning people are at their physical and mental peak between seven and eleven in the morning, and night people are at their peak between seven and eleven at night. Sadly, the office generally isn't open between seven and eleven at night, so we all know which group are keeping the economy moving single-handed.

If you don't think anything will get you up in the mornings, simply have a small child. Then you will be able to get up quickly and efficiently, and you'll be able to do this six or seven times every night.

How to... get up really early

A handful of people only need three hours sleep a night. They spend the other five hours searching everywhere for people they can tell about how little sleep they need. Most normal people need twelve to fourteen hours in bed every day, not necessarily asleep but in loving proximity to the duvet.

Some people open their eyes and – ping! – they're out of bed and doing their yoga. There are very few of these people and thankfully they die young. For most people, getting up is a process of going through every stage of evolution from a lump of primordial slime to a hairy uncommunicative biped. The final bit of evolution to erect, tool-wielding *Homo sapiens* takes another hour in the bathroom.

There is a freemasonry among early risers. When you meet someone on the street before half past six it is obligatory to say 'Good morning'. This is a simple courtesy but also demonstrates that you're not just up at that time by mistake: you've actually got out of bed two hours earlier, cooked a full English breakfast, and are well into your day already.

For people who don't like getting up early, an early start for a holiday or business trip can be like a bad birthing experience. Deliberately setting an alarm for a time which features a six, five or even a four in the hour department is like turning the shower knob to the thickest blue part of the wedge. Ironically, once you've set the alarm for 5.45, you will then also see the clock at 1.35, 3.18 and 4.44. You will also see it eighteen times between 5.00 and 5.44 as you squeeze out every last wink of duvet warmth.

Getting up early in the summer is a cinch, as there's sun streaming through your window, larks singing on your window sill, and cornflakes gambolling in your bowl. In the winter, it's pitch black outside, your car is trapped in a block of ice, and you've got to cook porridge for yourself which you don't even like.

Getting up very early for work on a winter weekday is such a cruel and unusual thing to do that you're probably infringing your own human rights. When you have to get up early, the trick is to get dressed quickly. If you get into slippers and a thick dressing gown you might as well still be in bed because you've yet to go through the sickening naked bod with goosebumps phase.

The only away of alleviating winter wake-ups is to have your underclothes simmering on the radiator. Getting dressed is then like getting back into bed, except you're now standing up. You can also think about getting one of those nifty tea-making machines, generally called husbands.

How to... lie in

In life there are so few opportunities to lie in that you should take full advantage of them when you can. When you're a kid, you get up immediately because there's always some urgent scampering to be done. When you've got kids yourself, you get up immediately to stop the scampering becoming a full-blown riot. When you're old, you know that death is the ultimate lie-in so you might as well get up at dawn and creosote the fence while you still can.

Lying in starts with the decision that your bed is the closest thing to earthly paradise and that you're going to stay in it. If it's a Saturday morning, a school holiday or the day after your tutorial, you can just turn over, make a little purring sound in the back of your throat and slip back into a warm fug.

However, it is possible to get up and still have a lie-in. If you keep your brain in sleep mode, open one eye and stay firmly in your pyjamas, it's quite possible to feed the baby, worm the cat, make the tea, get the papers, cook a full English breakfast and still go back to bed afterwards to continue your lie-in.

The rule is that there must be some trace of vestigial body warmth under your duvet for the lie-in to continue. If you've done so many of the household chores since getting up that your bed has gone stone cold, then, technically, when you get back into it you are having a nap.

Never take dreams you have during a lie-in seriously. The marsh-like gases you are breathing during the second or third hour of your lie-in have the same hallucinatory effect as a small tube of glue.

Students are the acknowledged masters of the lie-in. Honours students can sleep well past midday without batting an eyelid. For media studies students this is often the intellectual high point of their course. Lie-ins are all relative: for a farmer to be still in bed by the end of the shipping forecast is an epic lie-in by their standards, and cause for worried debate in the local farming community.

The bed fug is essential to the lie-in. This is the combination of warm air, warm body and warm duvet, and is the adult equivalent of being safely in the womb. A premature exposure to the world from either state can be deeply traumatic. Those wanting to endanger their relationships simply have to whip the duvet off their beloved and leave them looking like a shivering newborn rat. They will look like this for the split second before they get up and punch your lights out.

How to... get dressed

Getting dressed is a tricky business, and the worst time to attempt it is first thing in the morning. The brighter and more colourful the clothes you wear, the earlier you get up. Most evening people wear black because they are completely incapable of making colour-matching decisions before midday. On the other hand, people with fantastically bright colours get up too early, have to get dressed in the dark, and can only pick out lime-green tops.

Avoid colourful patterns in the morning as trying to accessorize will take for ever. (If a woman's wardrobe looks like a curtain shop you can guarantee she doesn't start work early.) You also need to think about the weather and cross-reference it with your office air conditioning. There's no point in going out in your woolly leggings if your office has the ambient temperature of Costa Rica.

As if getting dressed weren't difficult enough, you have to take your jimjams off first so not only are you befuddled with sleep, you are also numb with cold. There is a huge temptation to throw on the nearest corduroy skirt, which is why it's absolutely vital not to leave any corduroy skirts lying around when you go to bed.

Once you've got yourself suitably naked, you have think about underwear. For many men this is simply a question of stepping into the ones you dropped the night before, because until your pants are crawling into the laundry basket of their own accord they are still perfectly OK for use. Younger people often dress to be undressed, which leads them to wear all sorts of dangerous and impractical undergarments. Older people also dress to be undressed – but by a healthcare professional, which means they can relax in big, comfy pants.

The next big issue is whether to tuck your vest into your pants. This is made a lot easier if you're the absurdly macho type who doesn't wear a vest or, heaven forefend, pants. You can, of course, let your vest hang outside your pants, but this then leaves a VVL or visible vest line, which men absolutely dread.

Women often fling open their wardrobe first thing in the morning, look at serried racks of clothing, and then panic that they've got nothing to wear. That's because women dress to suit their mood, and they don't know their mood until they're dressed and by then it's too late. Men dress to suit their suit. As a fallback, everyone has one set of clothes in which they feel entirely comfortable. But it's worth remembering before you start looking for them that the natural home of that set of clothes is in the wash.

How to... eat cereal

Cereal eaters can be divided into those who eat high-sugar-content cereals for pleasure and those who eat high-fibre-content cereals as if they were packing explosives for a tricky demolition job. For the second lot, the key to cereal consumption is roughage and the most important statistic on the box is fibre content, which should ideally be the equivalent of eating rope.

What attracts many people to muesli is constipation. The advertising shorthand for this is Switzerland. Not all muesli eaters are dull people. Some muesli eaters put prunes on top of their muesli to add excitement.

Cereal itself is split between those you pour into a bowl and those you place in a bowl. Bisk manufacturers have been trying for years to get people to eat three at once. A lot more people would do this if you could fit three in a bowl. Sadly you can't, unless you put them on their sides, and then they'll be dry at the top and wet at the bottom.

The golden rule of cereal consumption is never let someone else pour the milk. The danger is they'll be a flooder, and before you know it your bisk will be floating around the bowl before disintegrating into a formless mess. That way muesli lies. On the other hand, you don't want dry bisk syndrome, where you can't actually chew it because it's stuck to the roof of your mouth.

Many cereals have a little plastic toy enclosed in the packet. This can be worrying if little Johnny accidentally eats the plastic toy along with his Weetybangs. On the other hand, the nutritional content of the toy is roughly equivalent to a spoonful of Weetybangs. Often, these toys come as one of a set which children are encouraged to complete. During the competition, the child's consumption of the cereal remains constant but the adult purchase of boxes soars, with the result that you end up with a cupboard full of mutilated boxes.

Inevitably, however many boxes you buy, you can't find Fidget the Lidget to complete your set. This isn't particularly surprising, as there is only one Fidget the Lidget in existence and it sits on the desk of the Weetybangs managing director in Minnesota.

The great thing about cereal is that you can eat it anywhere, doing virtually anything, which is why it's a bit of a surprise that most people choose to sit behind the packet and read it. By the end of a bowl of cereal most people have discovered what cereal Her Majesty prefers, what the daily recommend dose of zinc is, and why their life is incomplete without Fidget the Lidget.

How to... have a bad day

They say that bad days start when you get out of bed on the wrong side. If you have a wall on one side of your bed then that's probably true. Generally, bad days start by getting up either too late or too early – usually after having a vivid dream of something you wouldn't normally give headroom to.

On bad days you close the front door one second after realizing that your keys are on the kitchen table, and one second before you realize that the outer porch door is also locked. When you reach for your mobile phone you remember that you lent it to your partner who left for Swindon five minutes ago.

Bad days happen because individual bad things happen in groups of three. The grandfather and mother of bad days is when you lose your job, you phone home to get some sympathy and your partner says they're leaving to live with the person who just sacked you, and on the way home you crash your car into the back of the one person who was likely to give you another job.

Standard bad days are when you decide to work at

home on the same day that they decide to have the world convention of pneumatic drills outside your front door, during which it's necessary to cut off your water, phone and electricity. On the bright side, the postman will still get through to let you know your house is being repossessed.

When you're having a bad day you'll notice every tiny little thing that goes wrong, because these tiny little mishaps serve the purpose of 'just about summing it all up'. The good thing about bad days is that they make an average day seem great. The fact that the traffic that held you motionless for three hours yesterday is moving at 20 mph today seems like bliss.

One interesting thing about bad days is that they seem to last for ever. You can get three good days into the space of one bad day. The reason for this may be that bad days are self-perpetuating: something bad happens, you shout at somebody, and then something else bad happens courtesy of the person you've just shouted at.

A good way of avoiding bad days is not to inflict them on yourself on the first place. People put an elephant in their diary because it looks very small and manageable from a long way off, and then they wake up one morning to discover that they've got an elephant in their in-tray.

Bad days generally come along once every three weeks, with an absolute stinker once a quarter. If you're experiencing more than this, then there's probably something wrong with your life. You need to get this fixed, but make sure you don't attempt it on a bad day or you'll only make things worse.

IDLING AND POTTERING

How to... pass the time

We live in such a fast-moving society that when we are faced with spare time the first thing that fills it is panic. Spare time theoretically allows you to do all the things you've always meant to do, like sorting out your pension or clearing the guttering. Theoretically, that is, because this kind of activity actually requires as much planning, concentration and application as getting married. Three hours is not going to be enough time to find the paperwork/ladder, let alone do anything constructive, so why bother?

During a moment of spare time your thoughts may drift to people you haven't spoken to for a long time. You may even think about giving them a call or writing them a lovely letter. Before you rush into this, just remember that the inevitable consequence of this will be that you'll have to arrange to meet and catch up, and bang goes any more spare time.

You could go for a little walk. Don't make the mistake of walking off in the same direction as you would normally drive because you'll end up strolling along a dual carriageway. Instead, you must have a purpose for your walk: buying a paper is good; posting a letter is also good; writing a letter to the paper will give you two walks; forgetting stamps a third.

Many people with very little to do spend their spare time watching daytime TV. This is much like watching paint dry except not as colourful or useful. After three hours of either you also get the nagging feeling that it's probably time you went back to work, especially if you work as a painter. It's generally worth remembering that daytime TV is designed to work best with your vacuum cleaner on turbo-boost.

Very busy people are occasionally ambushed by spare time and are forced to stare into the dark abyss of their meaningless existence. This is where a dog can come in handy. Dogs have many faults but existential angst is not one of them. Once you find yourself at one end of a lead, you'll have a million and one things to chase, sniff, dig up, eat and pee on. It's like a fun version of real life.

Some people get a little bit overambitious with their spare time. Give them an hour without scheduled activity and they'll decide they're going to learn Spanish. That's why so many *Speak Spanish in an Hour* books are sold and why so many people speak an hour's worth of Spanish.

Retirement is like being given all your spare time in one big chunk. People either choose to work even harder than they did before, or just die and get it over with. Sadly, if you can't cope with a couple of hours' leisure time, you're going to find eternity a bit of a challenge.

How to... talk about the weather

Talking about the weather is the essential lubricant of social intercourse in this country. In Russia it's the bear hug and a bottle of vodka, and in America you have to give people a high five and tell them you love them. Be grateful for small mercies.

Entry-level chit-chat suitable for ladies in post offices is either 'Lovely day' or 'Horrible day'. Don't bother with anything in between like 'Overcast day'. If there's nothing worth commenting on, go for the multi-purpose 'Changeable weather'. On the odd occasion when the weather is actually interesting don't make the mistake of talking about it even if it's 40° above or below freezing; allow yourself 'Hot/cold enough for you?' If it's moderately breezy, don't make a fool of yourself by running in yelling 'It's a twister!'

When you've exhausted the potential of today's weather you can move on to seasonal observations. The British have seasons but not in any sensible order; we often go for the *quattro stagione* approach where we have all four seasons at once, often on the same day. Similarly, we like to mark the start of summer with snow and the onset of winter with a heatwave. This allows us the luxury of saying 'We didn't really have a winter/summer' all through the following spring/autumn.

Dull, grey shoe-wearing people have a numbing capacity for remembering patterns of weather stretching back many years. When you observe that it seems cold for the time of year, their standard response will be, 'It was minus twenty this time last year/five years ago/the year of Suez.' Always counter this with, 'Yes, but 1792 was the real shocker'.

Never get technical about the weather: no one, especially forecasters, knows what a front is. (One of the most bizarre national pastimes is tapping barometers without knowing why.) Bumping into your neighbour and commenting that it looks like an occluded front on the way isn't small talk, it's crazy talk and it will be the last you see of them for fifteen years. Rather, you should try to use local folklore, such as 'There's a lot of berries on the holly, blossom on the blackthorn, spit on the cuckoo' and so forth. Whatever it is, you can safely say that we're in for a bitter winter. Even after the mildest winter in living memory they'll hardly be knocking on your door demanding a retraction.

How to... wait

The worst part of waiting is the waiting. They say that a watched kettle never boils, but this is only true if you're so intent on watching it you forgot to turn it on in the first place.

In general, it takes a long time to master the art of waiting. There are three kinds of waiting: waiting your turn, waiting for an operation, and waiting for your prince to come. It's often the way that just when you think it's your turn for the operation, your prince comes and you have to make an instant decision whether you want to get married or have your gall bladder removed.

Some people don't mind waiting because they have the patience of a saint. It's worth clarifying that this generally refers to the patience of St Ralph the Long-Suffering not the patience of St Kevin the Hot-Tempered. Other people love waiting because it gives them a tailor-made excuse not to be doing anything else. These people spend their entire life waiting for something to happen. When you eventually die you may find yourself in a big waiting room. This isn't the waiting room for the final judgement. You have already been judged and you're in hell. If in doubt, check for the huge piles of *Woman's Realm*.

Waiting is actually a popular sport. At the top of the heap are ladies-in-waiting. Currently there is a ten-year waiting list before you can even start waiting. Often in life, you'll hear clever people referring to something called the waiting game. This is where you wait around to see whether you've been beaten. If you haven't, then you've won.

Waiting rooms are where people wait. When you first arrive in a waiting room always check that the door through which you're expecting to go isn't just a door in another waiting room through which other people are also expecting to go. The only difference between your living room and a waiting room is that you're not expecting anything to happen in your living room. A possible exception is when you have teenage children and then your living room becomes the waiting-up room.

On average 12 per cent of every adult life is spent waiting. Naturally a persistent question in life is 'Why are we waiting?' The answer is because somebody is keeping you waiting, and the reason why they're doing that is because whatever else they're currently doing just can't wait. So the secret to reducing overall waiting time is to be one of those things that just can't wait. The traditional options for things that can't wait are time and tide, which wait for no man (they wait for women, but then they take longer to get ready).

How to... read a Sunday paper

When you get your Sunday paper there is always a bit of argy-bargy as to who is going to read the news bit at the front; the rule is that if you've gone to the newsagent, you get to read it first. If you have it delivered, you're allowed to read it first if you go downstairs and make the tea. If you don't get the news bit first, you can read the human interest section with important issues like gender stereotyping and discrimination. Or, if you're a bloke, you can read the section on sport and motoring.

The next thing you do is pull out the jobs section: if you're looking for a job, you spend all Sunday checking through it with a fine-tooth comb; if you're not, you just look at a couple of jobs and see what Chief Operating Officers for Kent County Council are currently earning and how it compares to what you're on. You briefly consider a career in local government and then remind yourself that most jobs advertised have driven the previous occupant to resignation or suicide.

When you've flung that section over the back of the sofa you then pull out the children's colour section and give it to your partner saying, 'Here's your bit.' This joke must be repeated consistently over a twenty-year period to be really effective. There will also be a section which includes the symbol @: this gives warning that it involves graphic scenes of websites and computers. This ever-larger section is dedicated to showing just how close we are to the digital paperless society.

Colour supplements are always grabbed quickly under the mistaken assumption that there is something in them. Colour supplements would be better named sofa supplements, as 99 per cent of them are large colour ads for expensive sofas, followed at the back by smaller colour ads for sofas all at exactly £499. There are three other things in this section. At the front there will be two people talking about each other, and at the back there will be somebody talking about themselves. (In the tabloids one or more of these humans will be replaced by an animal.) Finally, there will be four pages of colour photos involving sex and violence in some new and relevant combination – quite often involving sofas.

How to... potter

Pottering is the most fun you can have in slippers. The essence of pottering is to do things that don't really need doing. Pottering often starts with a little light cleaning: you put a telephone directory away, find an old photo and, before you know it, you're in the attic looking through your old albums.

Starting is the hardest part of pottering as it requires shifting down to a gear generally used only in old age or convalescence. However, once you've accepted that there really is nothing urgent to do, that there is nothing on television that requires watching and nobody likely to need your attention, then you can give in to the potter.

There is a uniform that should be worn for pottering. Slippers or very old soft shoes are a *sine qua non*; cardigans or other chunky knitwear are *de rigueur*; and corduroy trousers or tracksuit bottoms are *Ich bin ein Berliner*. That's why you have to be absolutely sure you won't be disturbed while pottering, because you don't want to be caught looking like the bag lady of Bognor.

Men have traditionally been absolute masters of pottering, which is basically constructive idleness. They even have a shrine to it called the potting shed. Men can spend hours, if not days, sorting screws into different sizes, labelling creosote tins, and fitting old carpet tiles to the floor. In fact, they get so absorbed in this that it's almost impossible for them to give up any time for trivial matters such as gas leaks in the house.

As women do most of the housework anyway, their pottering focuses on not doing little things around the house and tends to concentrate on packets of chocolate biscuits which, because they have been started, need to be finished. This is done while reading an old magazine, preferably with a juicy article about the dysfunctional family of a soap star. A packet of biscuits dunked in an oversize mug of tea can last up to an hour, especially if you only eat one at a time.

If you're not sure how to get your pottering under way, try the second drawer in the kitchen – not the one with the cutlery, but the one with the fuses, Sellotape and instructions for the microwave. Make yourself a nice cup of tea and then tidy this drawer. Once you find an old set of keys to a bike you no longer own, it's beginning to rain outside, and you've got the radio playing quietly in the background, you have achieved the quintessence of potter.

How to... collect things

There are two types of collections: fascinating artefacts of great variety and beauty such as your own collection, and the heap of old rubbish that is someone's else's collection. Generally, men are more interested in collecting than women. That's because they are hunter-gatherers and there is still a primal satisfaction in hunting down, subduing and bringing home in triumph a small blue Victorian medicine bottle.

There is a very fine line between collecting and hoarding. Some people will have cupboards packed with jam of all sorts, neatly labelled and ordered, but no one would call them a jam collector. The rule is that if you eat your collection you're not a collector. In fact, any kind of consumption rules you out: licking stamps is a big no-no or, heaven forbid, posting a valuable letter. Spotting a train and then actually catching it is a heinous crime among trainspotters.

There are three parts to every collection. First, there are the things themselves, which have to be in close proximity. One toby jug in your house and another toby jug in your neighbour's house isn't a collection, it's two individual toby jugs leading their own separate lives. That's why the second vital part of any collection is the display unit, album, notebook or shallow mahogany drawers. Once the collection is in one place, it allows the third and most important part to come into play: the system. This is the index, catalogue, order, schema or overarching theoretical construct that gives meaning to your five Matchbox cars.

On a simple level, people collect things in order to impose order on a chaotic world. Obsessive collectors often have chaotic lives. But then you're unlikely to develop satisfying personal relationships when you've filled your house full of half a million two-inch Napoleonic lead soldiers. You're also likely to have a severe case of lead poisoning.

It is an immutable law that people collect what is subconsciously lacking in their lives: stamp collectors lack communication, trainspotters lack power and direction, beer mat collectors lack drinking partners, rare football programme collectors lack rare football programmes. Saddest of all are rare birds' egg collectors, who have no beauty or value in their own lives and feel the need to steal it from the most beautiful and valuable of species.

One of the dangers of collecting things is if you accidentally get a full set. This could expose a gaping void in your life, but fortunately collectors have found a way round this. It's called micro-specialization, where you concentrate on an ever more tightly defined area.

The downside of this approach is that you become the only person alive collecting this micro-speciality, which means you rapidly complete your collection again. The final desperate solution is that you have to put away your stamps and start collecting stamp tweezers.

How to... do a jigsaw

Jigsaws are the attempt by the powerless to impose order on a chaotic universe. That, or they're a selection of funny-shaped pieces that you fit together. Jigsaws are like bottles of tranquillizers. They make the same sound when you shake the packet, they calm your nerves, and generally you don't finish the whole lot in one sitting unless you're very depressed.

The standard jigsaw piece shape with its combination of sad mouths and jug ears is designed to restrict pieces to one precise location so you can't just plonk them down and pretend that the final picture is supposed to look like a surrealist collage. Jigsaw pieces are designed to fit together snugly. The use of a hammer, glue, scissors or any other household implement should suggest to you that the piece would probably be happier somewhere else.

Once you get over 200 pieces you're in serious jigsaw territory; 1000 pieces will keep an average adult off the street for three days; and a 5000-piecer is the equivalent of a thirty-day custodial sentence. Research shows that at any one moment in the UK there are more people working on jigsaws than in manufacturing industry.

People get very retentive about their jigsaws. If someone has spent the last four years doing a 5000-piecer of the Norfolk skyline, the last thing they want is you to wander by and slot in an odd seagull. It's not much fun doing the same jigsaw over and over, so you need a continual flow of fresh puzzles. One important word of warning: never buy a jigsaw from a charity shop as they always have three pieces missing.

If you've ever wondered why you have a dining-room table with six matching chairs when the combined total of your family and friends comes to well under that, it's because that's the only place in the house where you can do a jigsaw unmolested. One tip. Make sure your table is actually bigger than the final jigsaw or you'll have to do one of the edges on a separate side table, which won't impress anybody.

The picture of the jigsaw affects the difficulty. Blue sky over empty sea is every jigsawer's worst nightmare, especially if for some reason the puzzle comes without any edge bits. Without any picture to go on, you have to test every bit in every position, which is the equivalent of the work of the Enigma code breakers in the last war. It's frightening to know that 2 per cent of the population over seventy are currently engaged in work of this nature. Maybe they think what they're doing is of national importance. If it's keeping them off crack cocaine, perhaps it is.

How to... have a shed

A shed is to a man what a handbag is to a woman. It's an intensely private space that contains all the essentials for surviving the modern-day world. In the same way that no decent man would ever consider delving into a woman's handbag uninvited, no reasonable woman would dream of setting foot in a man's shed.

Women's handbags smell of copper, leather and lavender. Men's sheds smell of petrol, creosote and rust. You wouldn't expect a lady's handbag to smell of petrol and creosote, and you'd be right to be deeply suspicious of any man whose shed smelt of leather and lavender.

The soul of the average British male is on display in his shed, which is why a decent padlock is one of the first requirements. Every shed must have a spade and, however full the shed is, it must be accessible without actually stepping inside the shed. All sheds must have a miniature filing cabinet full of meticulously sorted and graded screws and nails. No one knows where these screws and nails have come from, and no one knows where they will go. Their purpose is simply to be graded and meticulously filed.

Old tins sprout in sheds like mushrooms and, like mushrooms, many are extremely toxic. The tin selection must include woodstain and varnish which have been used once for the initial staining and varnishing and never again.

The lawnmower has pride of place in the shed, in the same way that the purse has pride of place in the handbag. That's because it is a symbol of independence and power over the vagaries of the outside world. Never comment on the size of another man's lawnmower.

The golden rule in a shed is never put something on the floor which you can hang from a wall. Onion sets, rakes, bicycles, canoes can all be hung, and are all improved organically/mechanically by the experience. Remember, though, that real men don't suspend their lawnmowers, in the same way that real men don't wear thongs. If it's hangable, it's a little plastic hairdryer and not a real lawnmower at all.

Sheds either have a large collection of potatoes or a large collection of pornography in storage. It's important not to confuse the two and walk proudly into the kitchen on a Sunday morning with a basket full of pornography. Similarly, it's best not too get too aroused by potatoes.

When you find yourself carpeting the shed and arranging for cable TV to be installed, it's probably time to check on the state of your marriage. If you discover that your wife is actually living with another man and has two new children by him, you're probably spending too much time in the shed.

How to... go for a walk

There are two prime motivations for walks: one is the need for fresh air, and the other is the need to get out of the house. It's interesting how the quantity of fresh air in a house drops in proportion to the number of in-laws also in the house. The only things you need on a walk are your keys and an old coat. If you find yourself packing a knapsack then you're in grave danger of rambling, which is an extreme sport for pensioners.

The old coat is one of the high points of going for a walk because its pockets are like a scrapbook of your past life. There will be one ticket stub from the time your old coat was a new, hip coat. Deeper in the pocket will be the back-door key which you have been fiercely blaming your partner for losing. If you're really lucky, there will be one sweet minus its wrapper. The protective layer of dirt and fluff can be removed with a few vigorous sucks.

Walks, however short, have to have an object, otherwise you wouldn't know which way to turn when you closed the door. The best destination is the corner shop, where you can buy something you've been meaning to get for ages, such as a light bulb for the shaving mirror or white laces for plimsolls. It doesn't matter if the shop doesn't have these items, because you'd only have to do something with them when you got back. Going round the block is a good option, but do check that your block is actually round or at least square. Otherwise you'll be walking for hours, and walks lose their therapeutic effect when you have to hitch-hike home.

On a short walk, you don't have to look at the view because you live in the view. Instead, you can look into people's houses and see what they're watching on TV. If you take a remote control with you, there's no need to miss your favourite programme. You can also look at the notices stuck on telegraph poles. These are mostly planning applications for an extension to number seventeen. This is often the first you'll hear of your wife's plans for your house.

One of the dangers of going for a walk is meeting somebody else who's going for a walk. You then have to perform the traditional shuffle and pass. This is where you make just enough small talk to work your way round the other person so that you can then edge away and continue your walk. If you've planned to go round the block, it's best to abort at this stage, otherwise you'll meet them again on the other side and you'll be perilously low on small talk.

How to... fish

The definition of an angler is a man who prefers British weather at its worst to his wife at her best.

Angling is the biggest participation sport in this country. In fact, the only non-participants are the fish themselves, who find the whole sport a bit beneath them (or above them, to their way of thinking).

It is a point of honour for anglers to have a vast amount of kit and then to carry it all on an ageing bicycle so that they look like a member of the British motorcycle display team practising a pyramid formation minus the rest of the team. The rod for the fisherman is the equivalent of a beach towel. Its main purpose is to tell other anglers which bit of the bank has been reserved. Its secondary role is to tell the fish where to avoid.

Anglers also have a huge net that looks as though it should be hanging over the side of a deep-sea trawler. This is to give the impression that a massive haul of fish is expected. In fact, all these nets are connected under-water to other anglers' nets so they can shuttle round the one little tiddler that's been caught during the day.

Many anglers will have a big plastic bucket full of wriggling maggots. This is usually an aid to interaction between anglers, who are notoriously deficient in the conversation department. Comparing wriggliness of maggots is an easy and non-controversial way of getting into conversation. The maggots are also the last historical evidence of the one and only time the wife provided a packed lunch.

Serious anglers spurn sparkling highland streams packed with trout, as this would be like casting into the fish counter at your local supermarket. Instead, they choose the most polluted, stagnant stretch of water, the theory being that the fish will be as keen to get out of it as the anglers are to get them out of it.

Fly-fishing is an advanced form of angling where you cast your line into mid-air and hope to catch a fly. It sounds difficult, but there is as much chance of catching a fly like this as there is of catching a fish. Fly-fishermen often wear hats covered with coloured lures. This shows just how often other anglers have cast directly into their hat and explains why fly-fishing is often classified as a dangerous sport.

You can often see anglers in pubs telling animated stories with their eyes wide and their arms flailing. That's because 90 per cent of anglers have never actually seen a fish and are enormously surprised when it doesn't come up in a thick, crispy batter.

HEDGES AND NEIGHBOURS

How to... have neighbours

Neighbours are the closest other people can get to you without having their clothes in your laundry basket.

The ideal neighbours to have are ones that you don't see, hear or smell. Neighbours from hell are ones you see, hear and smell far more than you want to. There is also the dangerous kind of neighbour that you get on so well with, you end up swapping husbands and having to move house in order to get away from the neighbours you used to be married to.

There are generally only two chances to meet your neighbours. The first is when you move in, and the second is when they move in. That's why there's a lot to be said for moving at night. The perfect balance is knowing the name of your neighbour but nothing else about them. The ideal conversation with a neighbour is 'Morning Brian, lovely morning,' especially where their name is Brian.

Over the past century the average height for a neighbour has grown six inches. Fences haven't grown during this period, and it's often the case that your neighbour can see every inch of your garden just by standing up. An Englishman's home is his castle, and his fences are his outer defences. Planting leylandii on the boundary with your neighbour is a formal horticultural declaration that you never intend to exchange a civil word with them again.

Neighbours used to be people from whom you borrowed a cup of sugar. This was actually as offensive as planting leylandii because a cup represented the entire family sugar ration for a month.

In city apartments you can have neighbours above and below you. A quick way to hate them is if you have to listen to their television and they don't even watch the same programmes as you. The rural equivalent of this is if someone's cow is in your field and it's not even the same kind of cow.

Some people get locked into a suburban addiction called 'keeping up with the neighbours'. This is because people who live in identical houses like to differentiate themselves by expensive accessorization. Often this is achieved by cars in the drive, the drive itself and the sophistication of the garage opening device. When buying a house, allow an extra 10 per cent on the mortgage for keeping up with the Joneses. If you are the Joneses, then allow an extra 20 per cent.

There is normally one position in your house from which you can see your neighbours doing things in their house. This can be the source of illicit pleasure until you realize that there's also the very same position in their house from which they can see what you're doing in your house. Go and borrow a cup of sugar and check it out for yourself.

How to...
Neighbourhood Watch

The chief aim of the Neighbourhood Watch is to keep an eye out for any suspicious activity. Often the first suspect is the old man wandering around peering into other people's houses. Before you make your first citizen's arrest, it's worth remembering that this person normally turns out to be a founder member of the Neighbourhood Watch on active patrol.

The Neighbourhood Watch generally see themselves as the armed wing of the parish council. Often the group is set up by a man who thinks that its main function is to have the entire neighbourhood watch him as he constructs a mini police state.

It's very easy to spot a member of the Neighbourhood Watch. First, they have the little Neighbourhood Watch sign on the door. The other fail-safe way of identifying members is by running an ultra-violet lamp over them. You will see that they have been invisibly marked with their postcode so that they can prove that they are indeed from the neighbourhood and not a prowler from a different postcode.

What the Neighbourhood Watch do best is to watch

the neighbourhood, normally from their front room with a cup of coffee, a pile of custard creams, and a telescope powerful enough to read what's on your bedside table from five streets away.

Neighbourhood Watch members have been trained to spot suspicious movements, often before they've been made. They are particularly keen to note down suspicious vans as these are the preferred transport of the criminal class, or working class as they are also known.

The Watch like to keep a keen eye on all aspects of the neighbourhood. While their dog is fouling the pavement, they will read the planning application on the lamp-post for an extension at number forty-nine and then mobilize the Watch to object to it in case it becomes a local crack den.

The logbook is the Ark of the Covenant for the Neighbourhood Watch. In it are recorded all suspicious or noteworthy incidents. In fact, any kind of physical movement is generally included. One of the big shocks of joining the Neighbourhood Watch is to find out that your movements have been recorded seven thousand times since you moved to the area and you have been intimately psychologically profiled to match known criminal archetypes.

Neighbourhood Watches are generally harmless, but you should start to worry when they require the wearing of armbands and the singing of marching songs. If you think things may be getting out of hand, the best thing to do is to set up your own Neighbourhood Watch Watch.

How to... garden

You can tell what kind of gardener you are by your tools: trowel and trug mean you're a primrose and sweet pea sort; wheelbarrow and seed dibber mean you're a potato and marrow person; concrete mixer and socket set mean what you most like to grow in your garden is a fourth-hand Ford Sierra.

Once you've been out in the fresh air for a few hours, you begin to feel a deep inner peace, which fades only after you've driven a garden fork straight through your foot. The best thing about gardening is that it gets you away from everyone else, which is why it's a little bizarre that people who've spent years on their gardens suddenly decide to open them up to the general public.

What real gardeners like most of all is fooling around with the compost. This is where you throw all your waste food to rot and be turned into rich nutrients for your vegetables. Of course, if you didn't grow so many vegetables in the first place, you wouldn't have so much waste food and you wouldn't be producing all this stinking compost.

The joy of gardening is that it allows you to go outside in your favourite corduroys and cardigan and pretend they're just your gardening clothes. To turn normal clothes into gardening clothes, simply mix with compost.

One of the best rituals of gardening is the bonfire, where you burn all manner of garden waste and a couple of your wife's dresses that you don't like. Done properly, bonfires should be huge piles of damp greenery with great choking clouds of smoke heading directly for your neighbour's washing. Remember, anything in the garden will burn, given a ratio of one piece of greenery to seven gallons of kerosene.

You don't need forty acres of prime agricultural land to become a gardener. It's amazing what can be done with a couple of terracotta pots and some window boxes. With care, you can feed a family of eight entirely on organically grown produce (once you've sold the marijuana from your pots).

Gardeners get pleasure out of growing things, but not when things grow without permission. Weeds can grow up to four foot high overnight, which is why gardeners actually spend most of their time slashing, burning, spraying, pruning and generally beating the hell out of nature.

The sign of a real gardener is that when they're away from home they think about their vegetables more than their family and, when they finally return home, the first thing they do is rush down the garden and check their

runner beans, totally oblivious to the charred embers of
the house.

How to... go to the tip

In a consumer society, going to the tip is the equivalent of going to confession. You certainly feel just as good afterwards, although it doesn't stop you going out and being a waster again.

The biggest and busiest part of the tip is the garden waste section. Look carefully in this skip and you can see what people hate having in their gardens most. Top of the list is grass. Some people will mow their lawn, gather their half bag of grass cuttings, and then drive fifteen miles to the tip. By the time they get home, the grass needs cutting again.

Everyone has something in the house they hate and can't wait to get rid of. This can be an old television, a big piece of wood with a nail in it, a lawnmower with a rusty roller, or a fat, grumpy and useless husband. The tip will accept everything with open arms except the fat, grumpy, useless thing. You have to dump him at the divorce court.

The tip is the one place where you really wish you didn't have a two-seater, open-topped sports car. If you've demolished a low brick wall, you'll have to make seven hundred trips to the tip with one brick in your glove compartment each time. People with big, ugly MPVs and hatchbacks positively glow with smugness when they start unloading four tons of mixed rubble from the back.

It is also the only place where normal British people will speak to each other uninvited, and dumping rubbish is the closest most people get to a sense of communal ecstasy. First, there's the pleasure of actually getting rid of your thing; second, there's the pleasure of physically throwing your thing into the middle of a skip; and third, there's the anticipated pleasure of going home and seeing that lovely empty space where the thing used to be.

Older people especially enjoy tips as they're a kind of licensed vandalism. They love the sound of breaking glass and almost vibrate with pleasure as they smash twenty empty elderflower cordial bottles into the bottle bank.

Hovering round every tip like gulls are a group of men who scavenge mechanical carcasses. Their business is to take the TV you thought was broken, recondition it, and then sell it to someone for them to bring back to the tip the following week.

There is one other form of scavenger at the tip. This is generally a man who has climbed into the skip and is desperately searching for the useless, tasteless piece of crud he threw away yesterday which turns out to be something of incredible sentimental value that's been in his wife's family for generations.

How to... mow the lawn

Every weekend in spring at least 50 per cent of British men go to mow their own personal meadow. In Mediterranean countries they have an outdoor life in the streets, terraces and piazzas. In this country we cover our public places with grass and then demand that people keep off it. Lawns and lawn mowing are a national obsession; there is now more horsepower in the nation's sheds than there was in the nation's stables a hundred years ago.

Many people with small gardens have an electric mower that hovers above the grass. Not surprisingly, this has as much effect on the grass as a large hairdryer and is akin to shaving by hovering above your face with a razor.

People who are serious about their lawns like to have something with a petrol motor and grown-up metal blades that chop small rocks to talc. These mowers stop for nothing – the deforestation of the Amazon is largely due to the native population getting their hands on petrol mowers and deciding to extend their lawns a little.

The only drawback with petrol mowers is that you

have to start them with a ripcord that requires the same upper-body strength as a medieval archer. The reason why petrol mowers tend to drone on all weekend is that once you've got them started you don't dare turn them off again.

There was a time when lawns were mowed with machines that you pushed, but you don't see many of these around now as the current generation find it difficult to believe that those little blades of grass can be cut without the power of at least four horses. There's also the sneaking suspicion that the many hours pushing wrought-iron lawnmowers up sloping lawns is what made your dad age so suddenly after retirement.

On really big lawns, you occasionally see men zipping around on little sit-on mowers. These don't actually cut the lawn, they're just a way for grown men to play with bright-red tractors. If we had our way we'd be out on our little tractors ploughing up the lawn, muck-spreading and planting winter barley.

The great thing about mowing the lawn is that once you've done it and put all the clippings over your neighbour's fence, you can put the beast back in the shed and then get back indoors where you can really relax.

How to... have a bonfire

Technically, fire is a rapid oxidation process, but it's actually a lot more romantic than that: you wouldn't ever invite someone to snuggle down next to your rapid oxidation process. Making fire is a lot like making love in that you have to rub two things together. It is perfectly possible to make fire by rubbing two bits of wood together, as long as you make sure that one of the bits of wood is a match and the other a matchbox.

People with no experience of bonfires seem to think you just have to hold a match to a log and – wallop! – you get a glowing fire effect. The only possible way of making this work is to have a log soaked in paraffin. You will certainly get the glowing fire effect, but it will also be flickering around your body, so don't try it.

Kindling is anything that will catch fire easily, such as pyjamas, curtains, mattresses and children's clothing. In the absence of household items, you can gather pine needles or little bits of dry moss and lichen. It helps to carry a book of country lichen to help you spot the right types. If you can't find any, then burn the book.

To get started, try screwing up some paper into little

balls, but don't screw them up too tight: think junk mail rather than job application rejection. Then arrange a little wigwam of kindling over the paper. Remember, there's no point lighting your little fire and then disappearing into the woods for hours looking for something to put on it.

Fires need oxygen and a gentle breeze is best for this, not a blustery gale that blows sheets of flames into your neighbour's decorative hedging. In the absence of a breeze, you can lie flat and blow into the heart of the fire to fan the flames. Take care not to do this when someone else is fanning the flames by throwing a can of petrol on them.

The smell of a bonfire is one of the top ten smells in the universe. Down the ages men have been drawn to the smell as it means warmth, food, and the possibility that their old slippers have been incinerated by their wife.

Remember, bonfires can give off a lot of smoke. A bonfire will give off smoke in direct proportion to the irritability of your neighbours. Whenever you have a bonfire, there will always be a neighbour who insists on putting their washing out. Go round and tell them to take it down as this can ruin a good bonfire.

It's important to make sure a fire is properly out before you leave it. The time-honoured way of doing this is to pee on it. For some reason women have yet to claim equal opportunities in this area, so it remains a vital male-bonding exercise. It's normally just after you've completed this exercise that you remember the baked potatoes.

How to... organize a village fête

In the summer months the villages of Britain are studded with fêtes designed to show that merciless commercial exploitation is not the preserve of the Square Mile.

If you're going to organize a fête the first thing you need to do is to catch your village idiot. You then attach the idiot to a public address system and get him to do a running commentary on the sale of every raffle ticket and every time the rat is batted.

Bat the Rat is the financial bedrock of village fêtes, and involves dropping a sand-filled sock down a short pipe and then whacking it with a stick before it hits the ground – it raises about £19 on a good day and provokes unimaginable brutality when combined with local cider.

If you're at a village fête and there are stands like Guess the Age of the Cow Pat, then your village is actually in the commuter belt for a major metropolis. If there are stalls such as Touch the Computer or Watch the Traffic Light then you are in the rural heartland.

The best part of any fête is the cake stall, where you can pick up a freshly baked cake for 25p which probably cost well over a pound to make. Unfortunately, this is such good value that it attracts the professional fete scavengers. When you arrive at the fête ten minutes after opening time they will already be leaving with their estate car loaded down with bedding plants and fairy cakes. There should be a rule that entry to the fairy cake stand requires that you first visit the Count the Flies and Bat the Rat stalls.

The place you often end up in is the St John's Ambulance stand, where you get your two aspirin for the horrific ploughing injury you sustained in the Blind Man's Tractor game. Also, remember to leave half an hour to watch the Cubs and Brownies do their carefully choreographed displays of unarmed combat, or whatever it is they do these days.

Take a moment to visit the second-hand book stall packed with old textbooks on caravan maintenance and property law. These are exactly the same books that turn up at every village fête and purchasing any one of them is the secret way you become a Mason.

The climax of the day is the raffle, when someone wins the lovely picnic set and deckchairs that you thought you'd laid out under a tree an hour before for your family picnic.

How to... do a newsletter

Newsletters fill the gap between newspapers and letters. Another gap newsletters fill is the bin. Newsletters are a primitive form of communication used by people who are unable to converse socially. The rule is that the more anoraky the subject matter, the more vibrant the newsletter. Which is why the Internet flourishes as a virtual newsletter for the socially challenged.

The only way to guarantee readership of a newsletter is to make sure that everyone who gets one is in it somewhere. This is so important that you should always have a little column listing people whose names haven't been mentioned elsewhere in that issue.

Some well-established newsletters carry small ads, such as home-made honey for sale from Mr Pottinger. This will generally be next to the full-length feature article about Mr Pottinger and his honey-making. Also check out the letter from Mr Pottinger about honey and the making thereof. There may also be an editorial discussing the role of honey-making in the local community.

Adverts generally cost about 20p per insert, with a generous discount if you promise to insert more than once. Sadly, newsletters don't get much advertising because everybody who reads them knows who you are and what you have to offer and would have already bought it if they had wanted it.

The rarest kind of newsletter is the third issue. That's because the first issue has all the news, the second carries all the corrections and apologies for the first, and the third has absolutely nothing left to go in it.

The newsletters that last the longest are the ones with the biggest editorials. That's because editors don't mind how much work they have to put in as long as the first two thirds of the newsletter are given over to their opinions. Of course, editorial opinions don't have to be limited to the subject of the newsletter. For example, it's wondrous how much the editor of *Handmade Lures* has to say about our membership of the EU.

Journalistic standards are exceptionally high in newsletters. That's because getting the opening time wrong for a jumble sale can mean the difference between a fund-raising triumph and a serious breach of the peace.

Digital photography and desktop publishing have revolutionized the quality of newsletters. It's easy to get overexcited by this technology and end up with the toddler group newsletter looking like a scaled down version of *Vogue*.

Printing is now pretty straightforward. You simply give it to the person who has the most powerful photocopier at work. In fact, photocopier repairmen estimate that 90 per cent of breakdowns are due to people trying to print twenty thousand newsletters on the office copier during their lunch break. Interestingly, the newsletter for photocopier repairmen is called *Jamming*.

How to... win on quiz night

Quiz nights are a way of paying and displaying your complete ignorance. For all questions, there are three possible answers: sad shaking of head with 'No, it's gone, I'm afraid'; confident and loud response of first thing that comes into your head, followed by look of mild surprise when you're a million miles off; head in hands and repeated obscenities as if your stupidity has suddenly become painful.

Be careful when you're choosing the name of your quiz team. Calling yourself the Intellectuals guarantees being knocked out in the first round by the Pudding Heads. In a close-fought match it will always seem that you're getting questions like 'What is the chemical equation for photosynthesis?' while your opponents are asked 'Did you drive here?' It's worth checking who's buying the quizmaster's drinks.

There are two types of quizmaster. There is the amateur who reads questions and answers directly from a book. It's easy to get confused this way, and at critical moments they'll tell you that the second person on the moon was Marie Antoinette. If you argue, they'll deduct fifteen points for dissent.

Other 'professional' quizmasters spend lifetimes compiling their own books of questions. Every time they find themselves saying 'I didn't know that!' they write it down, on the basis that if they don't know it no one else will. When you've failed to get the answer *Bismarck*, they will add that it had fifteen-inch guns in a tone that implies that this too is common knowledge.

It's very easy to shout out answers when you're watching TV, but it's much harder to do it in front of complete strangers. That's why you'll suddenly find you have no idea who the current reigning monarch is. Once you've had a few drinks not only will you not know the answer to the question, you won't even understand the question. The Pudding Heads who knock you out may have a stupid name but they'll all be sipping shandies.

Getting a question right on quiz night is one of the purest pleasures of modern living. The feeling of joy begins to spread through your entire being halfway through the question as you realize not only do you understand it but you actually know the complete and entire answer.

If the quizmaster then tells you you're wrong, you will experience one of the most painful humiliations in modern life. That's why you should never believe people who tell you that pub quizzes are just a bit of fun. People who are there for fun get knocked out in the first round. It's also a fact that 98 per cent of fights outside pubs are quiz-related.

How to... run a charity shop

Charity may begin at home, but it generally ends up in a charity shop. Charity shops are to women what skips are to men – convenient places to dump rubbish and salvage absolute bargains.

Shops are usually staffed by ladies of a certain age, generally sixty-three. These women have a marvellous way of telling you that the shirt which looks like the back of a deckchair is actually rather sweet and frightfully good value. These ladies are also responsible for security in the shop, and most are trained in unarmed combat with various techniques for silent killing.

Like other outlets, charity shops display the best of their merchandise in the window. Don't be put off by this. What the ladies who run the shop think is best and what you think is best are two completely different things. Besides which, the stuff in the window is likely to be hugely overpriced at well over a pound.

By far the best things in the window are the mannequins from past ages of taste. You can often spot wonderful eighties mannequins in cocky little postures. It's just a mercy most of them don't have their heads any more. No charity shop would be complete without a shelf full of dead, flattened shoes. There will always be a pair of very new-looking, high-quality brown brogues. You won't believe what a bargain they are until you discover that they are size four or size twenty-eight.

Charity shops are where airport novels go to die. You'll find them in the collapsible carousel. It's not meant to be collapsible, but don't forget that it, too, has been donated because it is comprehensively knackered. Here you will find early Robert Ludlums, Barbara Cartlands and even one or two Harold Robbinses. To one side there are a number of hardback books, including *The Magic of Salad*.

Fashion is the magnet for most charity shop customers. In among the belted safari jackets, green polyester shirts and crocheted long johns there is an occasional gem, such as a green polyester belted safari long john. This is the compost heap of fashion from which the most avant-garde designers draw their inspiration for next year's look. The marvel of charity shops is that you can be wearing next year's look today.

Sometimes you'll be shopping in a charity shop and you'll find an exact copy of something you've just bought in a fashion outlet on sale for 50p. The reason it looks so familiar is that it is in fact the one you've just bought, which has been unbagged, rehung and devalued by 500 per cent before you can say, 'That bag wasn't actually a donation.'

RELIGION AND POLITICS

How to... be religious

If religion is the opium of the masses then it's the one drug-related issue that's clearing up fast. Spirituality is the direct, online, serve-yourself way of getting in touch with higher issues and is as popular as ever. Religion, on the other hand, is the old bricks and mortar way of doing it and is dying out quicker than your local post office.

Finding religion is a way of giving your problems to someone else who claims to have all the answers. The reason why so many religious people seem so happy is because they are relieved not to have to ask themselves any more difficult questions. Instead, they can refer to their Holy Book, which is generally the Word of God. There are many different versions of the Holy Book, depending on which reporter was around at the time. You also have to remember that the Word of God has generally been translated through thirteen different languages. Would you trust the instructions on your microwave if you knew they'd come the same route?

Religions are all man-made: that's why there are so many of them. They all have different branding, different packaging, and broadly hold out the same promises – mostly of the sort that can't be upheld in a court of law. Like other products, each religion promises to make your soul whiter than white and to shift stubborn stains on your character. Once you pick a religion that claims to be the best, you are obliged to think less of other people's religions. This gives rise to all sorts of hatred and unpleasantness, which fortunately religion allows you to be forgiven for. All good religions insist that other religions are mistaken, and, of course, they are all absolutely right.

If you're completely confident that you're in the one true religion, then you might like to try out someone else's religion for a while. Of course, if you have any doubts, then it's best to stay at home and increase your level of fervour for your own religion. Fervour is religious alcohol in that it makes you feel better on the inside but look stupid from the outside, and it eventually wears off leaving you feeling worse than when you started.

There aren't many religions that are made by women. Women tend to concentrate on the spiritual side, which is something completely different and doesn't require the erection of big buildings. In fact, another good way of analysing what kind of religion you've picked is to see how they pick their ministers and how these ministers then treat people who aren't the same sex as they are. If you have your doubts, simply apply fervour and all will be well.

How to... go to church

A church service is basically aerobics in slow motion. You have to get up, get down, come forward, and turn around, all to background music, with a kind of Mr Motivator figure in front. You even get your own mini aerobics mat hanging on the chair in front.

For people who don't go to church regularly, following what's going on can be tricky. To help you out, they give you a selection of books and brochures and guidebooks on your way in. That's like having four menus in a restaurant – by the time you've decided what you want, everyone's moved on to the next course.

Singing in church resembles a slightly amplified chewing the cud. The organist will play the first verse through once. If it's 'All Things Bright and Beautiful', you're quids in. If it's 'Gone is Gomorrah's Glory', wait for the man with the loud voice to go in first and then follow quietly.

Hymn numbers are displayed in a little frame by the pulpit. There are only two types of hymn number: single figures and numbers around the four hundred mark. All the other hundreds of hymns are the back catalogue of one-hit wonders. If you have a peek in the three hundreds, that's where they keep the politically incorrect hymns where God is called upon to smite the unwashed heathen and unmarried mother.

A key part of the every service is the sermon. This is where the vicar proves to the congregation why he was right not to pursue a career in television. The sermon takes place in the pulpit, a raised area which allows the vicar to see the people sitting at the back. As the person at the back is very likely to be the same person as at the front, a pulpit is generally unnecessary.

Some churches have pews. They may look the same but they all have different names; from the front, they are Pew, Pew, Barney McGrew, Cuthbert, Dibble, and Grubb. That's why people who slip into services late and sit at the back are known in the trade as Grubs.

Most services have a bit where you are supposed to confess your sins. That's why church services are on a Sunday morning, so you've got a Saturday night's worth of sinning under your belt. If services were on Tuesday morning, you'd be confessing an extra ginger nut with your hot chocolate on Monday night.

At the end of the service the vicar stands at the front and sends you on your way and then, as you file out of the church, he's there at the back door to shake your hand and say hello. Now that truly is miraculous.

How to... be superstitious

One way of guaranteeing good luck is to nail a horseshoe above your front door. Sadly, when you're up the ladder trying to fix the horseshoe, every other member of your household will walk under the ladder, which is slightly counterproductive. Black cats are witches' familiars and are therefore bringers of bad luck if they cross your path. If they cross in front of you when you're behind the wheel of forty-ton truck, it may be the cat's turn for some bad luck.

There are a lot of superstitions surrounding weddings. For example, it's often considered unlucky to marry. Even before you get married there are lots of things you have to bear in mind. For example, a single woman who sleeps with a piece of wedding cake under her pillow will dream of her future husband. She will also severely irritate the man she's in bed with at the time.

Some superstitions have their basis in solid practical truths. They say if your nose itches you will be kissed by a fool. That's because your nose itches when kissed by a man with a beard, the distinguishing mark of village idiots down the centuries.

NEVER HIT A JELLYFISH WITH A SPADE

Breaking a mirror brings seven years of bad luck. Interestingly, no shops offer a seven-year warranty on mirrors, so there must be some truth in it. Chimney sweeps are very lucky and are often invited to weddings to bring good fortune. In real life, merchant bankers are a lot luckier than sweeps, but for some reason no one wants them at a wedding.

Many traditional superstitions have died out. They used to say a fish should always be eaten from head to tail, but when you're faced with a fish finger this can prove problematic. Nevertheless, it's worth remembering that crossing fish fingers on a plate is very unlucky. A four-leafed clover will bring luck, but genetically modified maize is bad news. There seems to be some discrepancy there.

There are a lot of superstitions regarding salt. If you spill salt this is considered unlucky and you should immediately throw red wine over it. Similarly, putting salt on your chips before the vinegar is considered very bad luck in some parts of Somerset. In Cumbria the reverse is true. Marriages between men from Somerset and women from Cumbria are, not surprisingly, doomed to failure.

Warding off evil or bad luck can be done in a number of ways. A scientific education is one, but not walking on the cracks in the pavement is generally more effective. Touching wood is also good for luck, unless it's the inside of your own coffin – but by then your luck's probably run out.

How to... be new age

New Age people are new in the same way that the Ford Cortina was once new. Those that are still going are beginning to acquire classic status, but most have just rusted away or been crushed. In fact, the original New Agers are now reaching old age, which must be annoying for them.

New Age people wear sandals and always have long gnarled toes. This is their equivalent of Foothenge, and the sandal thong aligns exactly with the position of the sun at the summer solstice.

It's impossible to be truly New Age with a short back and sides haircut. The hair must have been allowed to grow unhindered from the first time the wearer realized they were living in the age of Aquarius. Hairstyles are frowned on and where absolutely necessary must conform to traditional corn dolly patterns.

On the other hand, having beads in your hair is the New Age equivalent of an Alice band for Sloanes. The beads provide a primitive calendar for the New Ager to keep track of how many days they have before their next wash.

The hardest part of being New Age is that you have to give up proper tea. Instead, you have to make tea out of things that grow in verges. No amount of sugar can make dandelion tea a good way to start the day.

After tea the next thing to go is meat, so being offered a cup of Bovril in lieu of the dandelion tea is not going to happen. Many New Agers are vegetarian or vegan. The worst nightmare for New Age Buddhist vegans is that they will be reincarnated as an Aberdeen Angus.

The worst part of being New Age is that your dancing is absolutely rubbish. Generally the influences are whirling dervish, tantric trance and a hint of pixie. A group of New Agers dancing together, seen from above, describes patterns almost identical to crop circles.

New Agers are great believers in traditional religions, as long as the tradition stretches back a few thousand years BC. For many the sun is a major focus of worship. It's depressing to think how many times the Druids must have gathered at Stonehenge for the summer solstice only for it to be rained off. It's probably why they packed it in and started worshipping something inside.

The ideal transport for the New Ager is yogic flying. Failing this, they tend to have a car, on the grounds that this is the only way they can get to the anti-bypass demos. Many New Agers retire to narrow boats, where they can escape the oppressive capitalist system and just drift along some of the finest achievements of the Industrial Revolution.

How to... meditate

The essence of meditation is to clear your mind of all the noisy clatter of everyday life and discover inner tranquillity. You can do this in six half-hour sessions at the local leisure centre, although parking can be tricky.

Finding the right place to meditate is vital. You should be as far away as possible from work, children, overhead power lines, traffic, shops, friends, computers and telephones. Strangely, if you manage to get away from these, you automatically acquire inner stillness and calm. Just don't ruin the effect by trying to cross your legs.

During intense meditation it is possible to leave the ground. This can either take the form of levitation, where you hover a couple of inches above the ground, or you can suddenly get excruciating cramp in your foot and fling yourself across the room in a desperate attempt to uncross your legs in record time.

Wearing loose, casual clothing is vital to meditation. Pyjamas would almost be perfect, except for the fact that it's difficult to clear your mind completely when you have the nagging suspicion that your bits are hanging out. Chanting can also be used as an aid to meditation. The constant repetition of 'om' can help induce a trance-like state, either because your brain settles down or because your flatmate has just punched your lights out.

Focusing on your breathing is a path to stillness and meditation. There is a special technique by which you breathe in and then, when that is complete, you breathe out again. It takes years to master but is hugely beneficial. The deeper the breath, the more beneficial the effect. Don't, however, attempt to make a phone call during very heavy breathing.

You won't get far in meditation without a guru. A guru is someone who can cross their legs more spectacularly than you can. Top gurus actually cross their legs behind their body. Interestingly, however good you get at retreating from the world, you can never seem to retreat from the guru. Especially if they've introduced you to a mystical technique called direct debit.

Meditation is often a pathway to Eastern religions. The stillness and inner peace is a very attractive part of these religions. Which is why it's one of the great mysteries that their adherents often feel the need to bang a tambourine in major shopping centres.

When you're meditating it's generally a good idea to turn your mobile phone off. Having said that, serious meditators can be in such a trance-like state they don't actually hear the phone ring. Many men achieve this trance-like state around the time of being asked to do the washing-up, walk the dog, get married, etc.

How to... be political

Everyone knows you shouldn't discuss politics at a dinner party because you'll only upset people. People who choose to go into politics full-time are therefore determined to upset people day in, day out. In a two-party state, plumping for one party or the other means voluntarily discarding one half of your brain. No surprise, therefore, that politicians often come across as halfwits.

You have to start really young if you want to get anywhere in politics, which means you miss the shift in life that always swings you from left to right or right to left as you get older. Often people become political because they want something better for their children; the reward for this is to have children who emerge at the far end of the political spectrum from themselves.

Budding politicians start at the local level, which gives rise to odd things like parish council expenditure on a park bench being debated on party lines with great passion, heat and venom. This is one of the main reasons why we don't have any park benches. At election time, political people put signs outside their houses. The intended effect is to instantly change the political persuasions of anyone walking past in the street. What really happens is that you suddenly get crossed off the dinner-party lists of people walking past in the street.

To be political you need to be able to talk with great passion, conviction and sincerity about everything except the answer to the question. You also need to show complete and unswerving loyalty to the party leader, whoever it happens to be that week. Finally, you need to have the common touch with the people (this doesn't mean sleeping with as many as possible).

There are only three kinds of people who knock on British doors: plumbers, religious nutters, and politicians – and they all promise to fix one thing or another. Unless you're very, very lonely, or have a problem with your washing machine, don't let any of them in. Remember, if politicians were really that useful, they'd be in Yellow Pages.

If you really want to change the world, you can take media-friendly direct action, or you can forget the direct action and own the media. The other route is to be very big in business and then buy up politicians wholesale. Of course, you don't give them money directly, but you do what no one else would do – invite them to dinner.

How to... vote

Politicians are generally people who don't have the personality to become accountants or the principles to become estate agents. The whole system would work much better if you could vote for whom you didn't want to get in. This would encourage politicians to say very little and keep very still.

Tactical voting is when one half of a marriage decides to cancel out the vote of the other half. If it weren't a secret ballot, most marriages would falter shortly after polling day. Some people like to keep their vote so secret they stay at home and don't bother voting at all. In that way no one will ever find out how you would have voted, except perhaps the Gestapo-types that eventually get in on 3 per cent of the vote.

The reason why there is such a low turn-out at most elections is because the polling stations are in places where people would never normally go – for example, the library. If they had the polling station up at the big house so everyone could have a good old nose around at the furniture, we'd all be up there like a shot.

In Britain, we have a great system where we all go into

the booth, vote for the person we most want as Prime Minister, and end up with some local village idiot as our MP. That's why Prime Minister's Question Time always sounds like village idiot feeding time.

Voting booths look like a cross between a urinal and a photo booth and everyone feels the urge to do something silly or obscene inside. In fact, that's normally the choice on offer. When it comes to voting technology we are still well ahead of the Americans. We use a small pencil to put a cross in a box.

When you get into the booth and look down the list of candidates you may be lucky enough to find someone called Steaming Pudding Brain III. It's one of the joys of democracy that barking nutters can put themselves forward for election. In some countries you won't find anyone like this on the ballot paper or, if you do, they'll be your only choice and you'll have to take them very seriously indeed.

In life there is a political puberty every bit as powerful as physical puberty. You suddenly wake up one morning and discover you're left- or right-wing. No amount of electioneering will change this, and you will vote left or right whichever chimps are currently occupying that end of the political spectrum. Strangely, people tend to drift across the political spectrum as they get older. But as their politicians do exactly the same, you probably won't ever notice.

How to... be on a committee

A committee is a small group of people who get together to dream up difficulties and avoid decisions. Anything that has a budget has a committee attached. In effect, it's a form of contraception which prevents the budget conceiving anything new and exciting.

A committee can't work if everyone hates each other. Sadly, this is the most common form of committee, because what happens is that one person gets on the committee and then their arch-enemy decides they, too, must be on the committee to stop them doing anything or having any kind of power.

The committee then divides into supporters of the two main people who hate each other, and discussions about even the tiniest details become divided into two camps. This kind of committee provides the model for the House of Commons.

Every committee has a chairman. This is a cross between a man and a chair that is only of any use when it's at the head of the table. The chairman of the meeting is the person most likely to have sympathized with the Nazis during the occupation, and certainly would have been first into the uniform. Anybody who volunteers to be chairman should be automatically excluded from the post.

Committees have procedures. These are designed to do three things: waste time, cut out any kind of fun, and reduce the will to live. It's perfectly possible to have a three-hour committee meeting that consists entirely of procedures without any actual content at all. It is an iron rule that the person who knows most about procedures knows least about anything else. Some people love being on committees. For the really keen there are subcommittees, which are little pools of procedural overspill from the main committee.

Minutes are the DNA of a meeting. The first half of any meeting is going through the minutes of the last meeting. This is like having the old meeting again, and it's a great chance to revisit the circular arguments that made the last meeting last until well after midnight. The person writing the minutes therefore has to be a combination of copywriter, diplomat and marriage guidance counsellor. If they were a lawyer they would be able to charge astronomical sums for this kind of work.

The agenda for the meeting is like a lighthouse in that everyone steers well clear of it. The real meat of any meeting is Any Other Business. In procedural terms, this is where the procedure stops for a bit and the vicious personal back-stabbing can get started. You can tell when something is really dirty when it's preceded by someone saying 'Don't minute this.'

How to... be a revolutionary

To be a revolutionary you need to start with an interesting arrangement of facial hair. Complete baldness is always a winner, beards are great (the bushier the better), and moustaches are fine but they must be a new and really odd kind that doesn't get repeated in history ever again.

If you can persuade people to take you seriously with a toothbrush moustache or a bird's nest beard or when you are a complete and utter slaphead, there's a chance they might also take your crackpot ideas seriously. Ugliness is no problem, as no revolutionary has ever moonlighted as a model for mail-order catalogues.

Make sure you're living in exile at the crucial moment. Anywhere's fine, except for America where the lifestyle tends to creep up on you and you suddenly find that you've become a revolutionary and charismatic IT consultant. Second, don't live anywhere that's undergoing a revolution itself as this can be quite off-putting. It's best to be somewhere like Switzerland or Britain, so when you're leading the workers in revolt they'll all be shouting 'Freedom!', 'Justice!', etc., and you'll be thinking, 'Let's get this place more like Switzerland!'

As a revolutionary you must be instantly charming to animals, children, peasants and workers, but for motivational purposes you must also be driven by a mass of sexual and social irregularities. Impotence is good as you can always get a feeling of power by incinerating the middle classes. Gross sexual overindulgence is excellent, too, as this always goes down well with the male workers and peasants (unless they're the ones being grossly overindulged in). Try to have at least one unspeakable vice under your hat to spice up later biographies.

Saying profound things is important. Any analogy will do. If every day you say something along the lines of 'Justice is a perishable fruit' or 'Liberty is the calling card of truth', something is bound to stick sooner or later.

The actual revolution itself needs to follow a strict pattern. First, fight in the hills or on a long march. Whatever it is, it must be uncomfortable for your followers and give you something to work into tapestries later. When you've decided on your facial hair, come down from the hills and man the barricades. It's no good manning barricades on suburban B-roads: they have to be near major tourist attractions for the photos, and near coffee shops for the post-match analysis. Finally, take power, wear a really dull uniform with nerdy headgear, and then usher in the revolution (optional).

How to... demonstrate

Very occasionally, the great British public get so annoyed about something they decide to demonstrate. This generally involves descending on London en masse, discovering how few public toilets there are, and then returning home with lots of shopping.

Chanting is an important part of any demonstration. The golden rule here is to keep your chants to words of one syllable. For example 'When do we want it? – Now!' is good. 'When do we want it? – Immediately!' is not. Having more than one syllable gives the impression that there is room for negotiation.

Placards are also essential. Don't bother with lots of standard placards as the television will always show the one witty one. Make sure you spell the witty placard correctly, otherwise you'll give the impression that the demonstration is by a bunch of halfwits.

If you're taking part in a youthful demonstration, it's obligatory to have one pretty girl sitting on the shoulders of her intense lover. This is how newspaper editors show what a big crowd it is. It also shows that if an attractive young woman is moved to demonstrate there must be something to it. Cute children carrying banners they couldn't spell, let alone understand, are also important. The one thing to avoid at all costs is a working man carrying a banner which says 'Pay Me A Fair Wage'. This isn't going to have any impact on anyone.

Civil disobedience is also a legal requirement of any major demonstration. To start this you need to park yourself somewhere where the police will have to move you on. The quickest possible way of doing this is to park on a double yellow line, which is the daily street protest undertaken by most city dwellers.

Once you've sat down somewhere inconvenient, it's important not to spring up just because you've been asked politely. After you've been carefully lifted away by bored policemen, you'll have enough of a story to bore your grandchildren rigid for years. Other people will do things like supergluing their head to the pavement. This isn't necessary unless you really feel very strongly indeed and don't mind losing part of your head.

Demonstrations should start in a big park, then go on to a seat of power via several tourist attractions. Of course, if you really wanted to have an impact you'd sit down in the fast lane of the M25, but it's not so much of a day out. Finally, you have to have a certain number of people in a demo. Eighty people might seem like a lot when they're in the village hall, but in London that's the normal number of people in a tube station lift.

TEENAGERS AND STUDENTS

How to... be cool

In between being a child and being a parent the most important thing to be is cool. However, it's incredibly difficult to be cool because there are no instructions to follow. You can't even decide whether you are cool – other people do that for you.

Simple things you can do. The first and most obvious is to stop enjoying yourself. No one with happy, infectious laughter is cool because the first priority of cool is to take yourself extremely seriously. Laughing is for people who don't get it. So start scowling and looking at the world with the attitude, 'Funny, I think not.' If you don't take yourself seriously, no one else will.

Second, ditch that jaunty walk. Cool people's feet never leave the ground as they are far too weighed down with the awesome responsibility of coolness. Get that spring surgically removed from your step and start shuffling. It goes without saying that cool people don't swing the ir arms. In fact, any sort of arm movement is a bit of a no-no as this could give the impression you are a Scoutmaster.

Never give the impression that you think anything

might be a jolly good idea. For example, going out to the cinema might be a jolly good idea, but if you're cool the last thing you would do is suggest it. Decisions like that are made through the sacrifice of the uncool. Only after the uncool have spoken and embarrassed themselves can the cool slump off to the cinema, even though this was the first thing suggested hours ago by an enthusiastic but uncool person who is now at home crying on their own.

What you wear is critical to coolness. Sturdy easy-care classics don't cut the mustard in the cool department. Cool clothing is always on the thin dividing line between what was absurd yesterday and will be ridiculous tomorrow. This line is slightly easier to tread once you have established that you are cool. You can then wear a bucket on your head and you will still be cool in the eyes of your less cool friends, who will all come out the next day with buckets on their heads. (This is how the fashion industry works.)

Fresh air and sunlight aren't good for cool as they make you happy and you have to remove your cool clothing. That's why cool people tend to sleep late and come out at night. However, just because it's dark doesn't mean you can't wear your sunglasses. Remember, all eye contact is deeply uncool as it implies a lapse in total self-absorption.

How to... be deep

One of the quickest ways of appearing deep is to say, 'Or is it?' after somebody else has said something. Or is it?

You can get a similar effect simply by transposing the key elements in any sentence. For example, when someone says, 'Women are the power in the home,' you could immediately reply with, 'Yes, but home is the power in the woman'. Just make sure there isn't anyone even deeper in range who then might chip in with, 'I think you'll find that power is the home of women'.

Humans, like fish, get more unpleasant looking the deeper they get. If you're going to be deep, don't wear bright colours. Deep people always wear black to signify their great undiscovered depths. Sequins have the opposite effect.

Including foreign phrases in your conversation is a *sine qua non* of being deep, preferably phrases nobody's ever heard of. You won't get away with '*Frère Jacques, dormez-vous?*' in all but the shallowest company.

Bitter hollow laughs are great for added depth. After someone says something completely innocuous, such as

'They're bound to have Hoover bags in the corner shop', a bitter hollow laugh will show that you know through long and bitter experience that life isn't that simple.

Even if you're proved wrong you can always retrieve the situation by saying, 'Yes, but is there a shop in the bag?' or *'Plus ça change, plus ça Hoover bag.'* Neither of these make any sense at all, but if you're sufficiently deep and are wearing black, people will assume you've found meaning at a much deeper level than they can penetrate.

Another excellent way of showing how complex and brainy you are is by answering any question with the phrase, 'It depends what you mean by that'. Don't use this too much, otherwise someone might just turn round and say, 'What do you mean by meaning?' You'll then be at such a depth that your head might implode with the pressure.

A vital accessory for deep people is a difficult book, preferably by a Russian author specializing in poverty, misery and death. It's best to buy this book second-hand so even if you don't get past page two it will still look as if you're reading it for the fifth time for hidden depths.

It's equally vital to steer clear of any ball games if you want to appear deep. Juggling, bouncing, heading and dribbling are completely contrary to cool pensiveness. The other enemy of depth and those that live at that level is the word 'bollocks'. You can't change the word round, it doesn't translate, and even 'Or is it?' invites the final authoritative answer, 'Yes it is'.

How to... be hard

In the new millennium, young men have found a great new way of expressing themselves, and that is to be hard. The first thing you need is a hard walk. A jolly spring in your step won't do unless it looks like you're about to run up and slam dunk a basketball. For hard men it's vital that you walk with your arms slightly out from your body as if you had huge muscles under your armpits. Similarly, you must walk with your legs slightly apart as if you are transporting genitalia of rhinocerine proportions (it's impossible to be hard and pigeon-toed).

Hard cars need to have fat tyres and a big exhaust pipe. For the chronically hard, shaded windows are a must so we can't look inside. For all we know, they're probably sitting inside wearing a pink fluffy cardigan, but it's probably not worth checking.

Conversational pyrotechnics are not at a premium for the truly hard. All you really need is a variation on 'What is it at which you are looking?' followed by a punchline, which can obviously be a punch or, if you don't want to loosen your grip on your lager/dog/bird, a headbutt.

Fighting is a very important part of being hard. Distressingly, for men who aspire to hardness, fighting can actually hurt quite a lot and not necessarily turn out to your advantage. On balance, it's much better to talk loudly about it. This means you can accidentally brush against someone in the shops and then turn it into an epic street scrap when you're talking to your mates.

You would have thought that really hard men would want to find a really hard woman to go out with. Far from it. They usually go for something really soft and fluffy to emphasize their own hardness. It's their way of saying they've outsourced their feminine side.

Tattoos are a great short cut to hardness, unless you have it done on your stag night and come out with 'Derek is my darling' on your right bicep. Having 'I love Mum' is perfectly acceptable for the clinically hard and does not imply in any way that your are a mother's boy. Again, not worth checking, especially if the tattoo is on the face.

Muscles and weapons are the currency of hardness, and generally you have one or the other. Small men with no muscles have very sharp, pointy knives which they like to exhibit at regular intervals. Bigger men like to accumulate muscles and then exhibit them in tight-fitting T-shirts. Remember that this is a private exhibition and not one to which you're invited and you may be asked what it is at which you are looking.

How to... fight

Most men have never been in a fight and wouldn't know what to do if they were in one. An extra firm handshake or a particularly snitty email is the closest modern man gets to naked aggression. Litigation is the modern equivalent of taking someone outside. The only difference is that you have to pay through the nostrils to do it and it's almost impossible to make up after you've done it.

When you're in a real fight you have to distinguish between a pushy-pushy fight which is done for pecking order purposes and a fight to hurt the other person. If you're doing a lot of talking and constructing elaborate insults involving parentage/sexual orientation/rearrangement of body parts/imminent visits to hospital, you're in the former. If you're grabbing a weapon, you're in the latter. By the way, even the sauciest insult is no protection against a swinging fire extinguisher at head level.

Proper fights have no rules. It's a dead give-away when nice chaps attempt to fight, because they put up their fists. This allows complete and unrestricted access for the boot that is making its way swiftly to the groin.

On TV when someone punches someone else there is the sound of a barn door slamming. You won't hear this when you actually punch someone, mainly because you'll be shouting very loudly, 'Bloody hell, I've broken my hand!'

The headbutt is a very strange thing to do in a fight. After all, many of the things you most want to protect are in your head. Headbutting makes as much sense as trying to clobber someone with your testicles. If someone does attack you with their head, don't respond by attacking their head, as this is likely to be their least sensitive bit. Remember that the most sensitive part of a man is generally his ego.

Sports can often lead to fighting. Rugby is virtually an organized fight, maiming is commonplace in badminton; and there are many horrific stories of Pringle rage in even the swankiest golf clubs. Boxing can also lead to fighting unless it's organized by a professional promoter.

Getting out of a fight is much more difficult than getting into one. Once you've got someone in a headlock, what are you supposed to do with the head? Honour is satisfied if you both grab each other's scruffs and then push one another away, a lip curled. At this stage, it's very handy to have someone standing close by telling you that your opponent isn't worth it. Be very careful not to pick a friend who thinks that everyone is definitely worth it and you should get stuck in immediately.

How to... reorganize your room

Reorganizing your room is a cheap form of therapy, if you discount the cost of physiotherapy to rebuild your back after the attempt to move your bookcase with all the books still in it.

The first thing to move is your bed. You can try having this directly under the window, which has the benefit of being able to kneel on your bed and watch the world go by. The disadvantage is that the world can watch you in bed. Also, during the winter, cold air will drop down from the window onto your chest and you will catch your death of cold. Having said that, you rarely hear coroners announce that the deceased caught their death of cold through going out without a jumper or leaving a window open, so it might not be a big problem.

The most foolish/rebellious option is to have your bed wedged against the door. This allows you total privacy but can be constraining when tea is ready. Other bright ideas which don't last are first, having your bed diagonally, unless you have a lot of other triangular furniture, and second, having your bed in the middle of the room. If you have no headboard, this feels uncommonly like lying on your own funeral bier.

Moving your wardrobe should only be attempted when you're really serious about changing your room. You should be especially cautious when it's a built-in wardrobe. Moving your wardrobe involves putting the entire contents on your bed. Beware of getting distracted into a sorting out your clothes session, as you can easily run out of reorganizing steam when your clothes are nicely sorted but the actual wardrobe is still in the middle of the room.

When reorganizing, be careful not to overdo it. If you find yourself moving floorboards, plumbing or load-bearing walls, you're probably going too far. There's also very little chance that you'll be finished before bedtime. Remember, the authority figure in your house – parent, spouse, warder – will always arrive at the exact halfway point between everything being neatly in one place and everything being neatly in another.

One of the major limitations in shifting rooms around is what you can move by yourself. Nevertheless, it's amazing what one person can shift using improvised broom-handle levers, ramps and a complex series of baked-bean-tin rollers.

When you've finally completed moving the furniture around, you should make one final check to see where the lights, plugs and telephone jacks are. Then simply make the final adjustments to make sure everything is lit, powered and connected, and – hey presto! – your room is back in the exact arrangement in which it started.

How to... shave

One of the reasons so many men go through the appalling rigmarole of shaving every morning is because not shaving would inevitably lead to the even more appalling rigmarole of being a man with a beard.

Because shaving is not one of life's most uplifting activities, some men don't bother for a couple of days and go for the stubble look. The impression they think they're giving is rough, tough man from the prairies. The impression they're actually giving is grubby little skanker. For their partners, a stubbled kiss is like having a Black & Decker sander pressed to your face for a couple of minutes.

There are now all sorts of gels, oils and creams available to help you shave. Oils are good because you can see where you're going, but they're also very slippery and before you know it your ear will be quietly bleeding on the floor. Creamy lathers applied by badger-bristle brushes are great for doing it like your father did it, but if there's one species who should be keeping their bristles it's badgers. Gels are good because they go a long way – generally over nearby curtains as they tend to be highly pressurized.

Never Hit a Jellyfish with a Spade

Why anyone ever used a cut-throat razor is an absolute mystery; it's like driving a hit-tree car or wearing a make-baby condom. Disposable razors are so called because they take up a huge proportion of your disposable income. These razors have two, three or even four blades on the same head, and claim to cut so close you actually expose your jawbone. What they don't tell you is that you can get the same effect by doing a couple more strokes with your simple, one-bladed razor. To keep the skin taut when shaving you have to pull a range of faces, any one of which would have got you a thick ear if you had pulled them as a child.

Men are always slightly disappointed by how few shaves they get from an average razor. The first shave is fantastic, but the next one feels like a rusty hacksaw blade. What has happened in the interim is that your beloved has shaved both legs with it, which in shaving terms is the equivalent of deforesting the Amazon.

If someone threw aftershave in your face in the street you would quite rightly have them for assault with a deadly weapon, yet up and down the country bathrooms are full of the screams of agony of men splashing raw alcohol onto their tender, bleeding faces. The alternative is to put on a soothing moisturizer with extract of ylang-ylang. But if you're going to undermine your manhood to that extent you might as well grow a beard.

How to... be glum

The four horsemen of glumness are tiredness, boredom, rain and low blood-sugar level. Any of them can lead to minor glumness, while all four together can lead to the very serious irritable bastard syndrome. Glumness is a small thing, but it can change the world – principally into an awful place where everything and everyone conspires against you to make your life a misery.

If depression is a black dog then glumness is a wet spaniel. It's a temporary service disruption for naturally happy people. Glumness is generally triggered by a small thing going wrong such as missing a bus, stubbing your toe, or not winning a charity raffle for which you bought 80 per cent of the tickets.

You then say things like, 'I'll probably miss the next bus, knowing my luck'. When you get the next bus no problem, you then have to say, 'There's probably someone sitting on the top front seat, knowing my luck'. If things continue to go well you may start to struggle. 'The bus will probably get its top ripped off going under a low bridge, knowing my luck.'

Glumness simply won't allow the possibility of anything good and cheerful happening during its tenancy.

Being glum has physical symptoms. The first is scuffy slipper syndrome, which makes it impossible to walk around the house without dragging your feet. The second is whiny voice affliction which turns everything you say into a whinge starting with the words 'I don't', 'I can't', or 'I won't'.

For the glum person, nothing is funny. Especially not the things that normally make them laugh. Their normally favourite jokes suddenly seem pathetic and childish, as do all their friends and family. When dealing with a glum person there is an effective two-stage de-glumming procedure. The first is to avoid the glumster, as anything you do or say will be childish and pathetic. The second is to go into the kitchen and cook a hot meal. For entrenched glumness, cook pancakes for pudding. If that fails, they are either clinically depressed or your cooking is really rubbish.

A high-risk strategy for dealing with a glum person is to out-glum them. It's almost impossible for two people to be glum at once in the same room, because glumness only works through relativity. Seeing somebody else being glum makes you want to buck their ideas up, and this has the side effect of bucking your own ideas up. That's why successful comedians are often depressives. Not only do they make you laugh, but you're also glad you're not as glum as they are and that you have a girlfriend, a job and a life.

How to... separate the men from the boys

Inside, boys like to think they are men; inside, men know they are still little boys. Boys want to grow up fast and get what men have; men want to be young again and get what boys have. Boys want to build their bodies; men want to reduce them. Boys cover walls with girls and cars; men cover walls with primer and topcoat. Boys iron shirts to go out on the town; men iron shirts to go in on the train.

Boys don't respect women because they're too soft and girly; men like to keep their jobs. Boys talk about sex instead of doing it; men talk about sex when they're doing it. Boys hit their sexual peak at about seventeen; men hit their sexual peak at about 10.15 p.m. Boys think their parents are aliens with bad taste in furnishings who know nothing about parenting; men think their parents did an incredibly good job despite their bad taste in furnishings. Men plan families; boys tell their families.

Boys wear clothes that fit their individual personality; men wear clothes that fit. Boys have an aggressive, cocky walk; men take a cab. Boys drive small cars incredibly fast on suburban streets in order to meet girls and impress them; men drive big cars incredibly fast on motorways in order to meet finance directors and impress them. Boys love their cars; men love their no-claims bonus.

Boys spend weekends on motorbikes; men spend weekends behind lawnmowers. Boys play football; men watch football. Boys do their stuff all night and sleep all day; men do their stuff all day and sleep all night. Boys can drink eight pints and be unconscious by 11 p.m; men can drink a cup of tea and be unconscious by 10.30. Boys know that smoking is hard; men know that giving up smoking is harder. Boys have a laugh with their mates; men have dinner with Fiona and Richard.

Boys let off fire extinguishers; men fit smoke alarms. Boys have backpacks; men have Air Miles. Boys like leaving home; men like going home. Boys can do fifty press-ups and bench-press a hundred pounds; men can work fifty-hour weeks and bench-press a hundred thousand pound mortgage. Boys get angry and pick fights; men update their CVs. Boys know it all without the benefit of any experience; men let boys learn the hard way. Boys think the world is their oyster; men know there is no such thing as a free lunch.

How to... be a student

There are two types of students: mature students, and normal students. Normal students are not mature.

When you first become a student you have to decide whether your life is going to centre around coffee or alcohol. If it's alcohol, then you drink yourself stupid on a regular basis. This is a vital part of the education process. The first year has to be spent in the student bar where beer is cheap; the second year is spent between the off-licence and your evil-smelling digs; and the last year is spent in rehab, or the library as it's sometimes known.

Alternatively, you can meet other like-minded students for a coffee and conversation. Occasionally these groups will really whoop it up and pass round the chocolate HobNobs. Some people meet their spouse over coffee in the first term at university and do their essays holding hands. If a coffee-type student tells you they're dropping a lot of acid, you can safely assume they're studying chemistry.

One of the most liberating experiences of being a student is that you escape the oppressive tyranny of your parents (after they've dropped you and all your stuff off at college that is). Most people take the opportunity to chill out, but others make the mistake of taking themselves seriously. This means they either go into student politics or student religion: student politics is alcohol with anger, and student religion is coffee with praying.

Poor students have to live on baked beans on toast, although if they were slightly richer they'd still be living on a diet of beans on toast because that's the only thing they can cook. The name of this meal is 'fresh fruit and veg' when they speak to their mothers once a term to ask for money. Asking for money is a fine art for students. They have to choose their moment carefully and then adopt a heroin chic look so that their mothers will be appalled at how close to death they are (despite all the fruit and veg).

The golden rule for students is not to get too friendly with anybody in the first week, because if they turn out to be the coffee-drinking nerd from hell you won't be able to shake them off for the next three years. Similarly, if you can look back and clearly remember what you did in your second year, then you probably wasted it. Third year is different. This is when you do exams and job interviews where you claim to have done nothing but study and organize impressive things for three years. The thought of a job is too much for some people and they go into hiding, otherwise known as doing a doctorate.

How to... grow up

Growing up is so profoundly difficult that most people choose not to go through with it.

Losing in love is a vital part of growing up. First, you have to be convinced that the world has never seen a love like yours even though it involves a lot of time hanging around in coffee shops playing with packets of sugar. Then the love has to end so you realize not all women love you as unconditionally as your mother.

Next, there's the economic wake-up call when you can't find the tree on which money grows and you're forced to get a job. That's when peer-group pressure suddenly becomes what you feel in a crowded commuter train.

To grow up, it is essential to put your entire wardrobe in a backpack and go somewhere big on scenery and low on social security. On your trip, you will need to have a brief and unsuitable relationship, some form of bodily mutilation (tattoo, body piercing, bad haircut), and you will need to get shockingly ripped off by someone who is doing you the favour of showing you that it's a big bad world out there without your mum and dad.

Obviously, you need to leave home to discover that toilets are not self-cleaning, that the magical missing link between shopping and eating is cooking, and that your parents were not put on earth simply to embarrass you in front of your mates. There are also certain things you need to have under your belt to qualify as a grown-up: you need to be able to use an automatic ticket barrier without fear; you need to have refused a swig of cider from a plastic bottle; and you need to have 90 per cent of your toys in the attic.

Growing up is when you understand that you get what you give, not what you're given. Then you realize that you only get something if you've already got it. In work, love and money, everyone has a built-in credit status: you may not know what it is, but, like a low sperm count, it can profoundly affect your future. The really tough one to learn is that if you really, really want something you have to let it go (this doesn't apply to helium-filled balloons).

Finally, you can test how grown-up you are by your position in a double-decker bus: kids at top front; teenagers top back; grown-ups middle top; older adults bottom back; really old people bottom front. If you find yourself on the bottom right at the front, you have grown up to be a bus driver.

MIXING AND MINGLING

How to... socialize

Socializing shouldn't be confused with socialism. Socialists are the ones that like to meet people's needs, and socialites are the needy ones that like to meet people.

To socialize properly you need friends, and to get friends you need to socialize, so sometimes it's tricky to get started. Fortunately, there are associations to enable people who have no friends to meet other people with no friends. Principal among these is the Ramblers' Association, who work on the principle that if you keep moving you won't have to talk to anyone.

For those who don't like going out at all, soaps are a ready-made social life delivered to your home. You get all the advantages of having people to bitch about without having to deal with them in person.

Real mixing involves moving from one person to another – it's a kind of emotional promiscuity. Good mixers have a knack of saying just enough to keep you going but not enough to really satisfy you. They are the Cheesy Wotsits of social intercourse.

Alcohol is the essential lubricant for socializing. It's

no coincidence that religious orders which ban alcohol tend to have services in total silence. The great thing about alcohol is that after enough of it you don't care what anybody else thinks and you can then socialize with total strangers, police officers and concrete bollards.

Dinner is great for socializing unless you're on the end of the table – then you get to socialize with an empty space on one side and the back of somebody's head on the other. Some people like to socialize in great crowds of people. This is the homoeopathic principle of socializing, in that the more you dilute yourself in a group the greater impact you'll have.

Going out to drink beer isn't socializing, it's just hanging around with your mates. Drinking champagne means there's something important happening, so you're probably at a function. But if you find yourself drinking wine, ten to one you're socializing.

Similarly, you know you're socializing when you find yourself in the presence of a buffet. When you have a glass of wine in one hand and a plate of food in the other, the only way to get the meat off a chicken drumstick is to pick it up with your teeth and then shake your head vigorously. This gets you fed and clears unwanted company at the same time.

Very few people actually have a social life. Children have to go to bed, parents have to put them to bed, old people want to go to bed, and young lovers don't want to get out of bed. By definition, therefore, people with a social life are those who have a dysfunctional relationship with their bed.

How to... put people at ease

The essence of socializing is putting people at their ease. You can always get off on the right foot by saying, 'You're looking tired'. Life is tiring, and everyone feels they're either working too hard or not getting enough sleep. If they've just got back from holiday, you can always wink and add, 'You obviously haven't been getting much sleep', which is equally good. Never start by saying, 'You're looking well', as this gives people no opportunity to talk about how badly life is treating them. Besides, their rosy cheeks are probably the result of a horrific cocktail of drugs.

For people under twelve a good starter is, 'My, haven't you grown!' Under no circumstances use this one with women between sixteen and sixty. With men, the more relaxed you are with them, the ruder you can be. With really good friends you can say, 'How are you, you leathery old scrotum?' However, you won't make new friends by saying this.

Ask people what they think about things. The sad truth is that most people don't think, but they do like to talk, which they assume is the same thing. Some people have one or two opinions which they've worked hard at, polished up and relish the opportunity to trot out. Give them an opportunity and then remember not to glaze over when they take it.

Mirroring people's body language puts them at ease. For example, if someone is slouching you shouldn't stand erect as this makes them feel that you're passing judgement on them. However, don't take this mirroring too far. If someone's making a cup of tea, there's no need for you to mime making a cup of tea next to them.

Towering over someone is intimidating, so try to get beneath their eye level if possible. You can do this by sitting or crouching down, but don't be silly about it; when you're visiting someone in hospital, there's no point lying on the floor beside their bed. This is unlikely to make them feel comfortable, as they'll forget you're there for a start, and they will probably be spectacularly uncomfortable already after forty-eight hours' surgery.

The best way to put someone at ease is to make them feel superior. You can do this by admitting you're stupid or sad or unlucky (most people will assume you're at least two out of three already). The fastest way to make other people feel superior is to bang your own head quite hard against a low beam. This instantly robs you of dignity, composure and intelligence, and makes virtually anybody else look as though they've got their life completely together. If you're very tall to start off with, this also solves the towering above people problem for a few minutes while you're bent double clutching your head in agony.

How to... go to a party

Parties peak between the ages of two and seven, where the high point is cake. There is another peak between seventeen and twenty-two, where the high point is the snog. The final peak is between sixty and seventy-five, when cake makes a comeback. After that, the men start dying and the fun goes out of it.

There is no greater challenge in modern life than entering a party where you know nobody and everyone is locked into hugely enjoyable conversations with people they love enormously. You have three options at this point. The first and best one is to go home immediately and watch television. However, you will then be tortured by the thought that this was actually the party of a lifetime where you would have met the person of your dreams and drunk champagne with them until dawn (someone else would be drinking the plastic bottle of cider you brought with you).

The next option is to step confidently into the room, say 'Excuse me', and push past various groups as if you were just feet away from joining the group that's waiting so expectantly for you. Keep saying 'Excuse me' until you reach a wall and then turn round and make your way back. Do this until you meet someone else doing it or it's time to go home.

Option three is to hack your way across the room to the table on which the nibbles are placed. You then have to pretend to be enormously hungry and start eating chopped carrots. If there is nobody at the party you know, you will then eat more carrots than you have eaten up to that point in your adult life. If it's a bowl of Cheesy Wotsits, remember that you're likely to be covered head to foot in orange powder by the time you finish.

The nibbles table is the service station for party conversations, and it's often a good place to start chatting with people who are desperate to escape the conversation they've just come from. One good opening line is, 'Do you know, from the other side of the room I thought these carrots were Cheesy Wotsits'. Don't be surprised if this is also the last thing you get to say.

There are only three cool ways of leaving a party: you can leave it propped up by your mates; you can leave it with someone gorgeous on your arm; or you can pretend you're going on to a cool club. Remember, it's very difficult to pretend that you're going on somewhere exciting if you're sober, by yourself, and covered in orange powder.

How to... mingle

People are divided into those who can mingle and those who stand at the edge of the room like lemons, feigning an intense interest in the way the curtain is hanging. Mingling is a form of social sieving: it's a way for interesting people to meet other interesting people and for dull people to find the curtains.

Of course, any fool can start talking to someone. The essence of mingling is not starting talking to someone but stopping talking to someone so you can start with someone more interesting. The best way to do this is to introduce the person you're talking to to someone equally dull. Dull people actually love other dull people because it takes the pressure off them to be interesting and amusing. Once they've shared the code words, 'I hate mingling', they'll discover within seconds a shared interest in railways.

A core skill for mingling is being able to interrupt people. If you stand politely next to two people waiting for them to stop talking to each other, you'll just look as if you're some kind of UN observer. The trick is to remember that at least one of the two people talking to each other will be desperate to get away. You'll know this is the case because a millisecond after you interrupt, one of them will shoot across the room in a desperate bid for freedom. Just make sure you follow the interesting one.

Professional minglers know that you can't mingle and eat a cocktail sausage at the same time. That's why if you look for the most amusing person in the room, it definitely won't be the person who's got a glass of wine in one hand and their face in a paper plate of nibbles they're holding in the other hand.

If you're stuck with someone who's sapping your will to live, you can activate the ejector seat of any conversation which is a simple 'Would you excuse me for a moment?' You then move away as if you were going to do something vitally important. You can then just stand five yards away doing absolutely nothing, because the cast-iron rule with mingling is that when you've been demingled you can't remingle with the same person. Being the one demingled is always slightly insulting, however politely it's done. Saying to someone it was lovely to talk to them has the clear subtext that it's going to be much lovelier talking to someone else.

How to... drink cocktails

Cocktails are the liquid interface between alcohol and modern art. At least, that's the kind of rubbish you come out with when you've had a couple.

The ingredients in a cocktail can be divided into two very clear categories: those that make you fall over, and those that boost your vitamin C levels – in other words spirits and juices. Drinking piña coladas therefore gives you the satisfaction of knowing that you are getting your recommended daily allowance of vitamins as you lie comatose with your head wedged under the footrail of the bar.

All sorts of fruit are used in cocktails, and the more exotic they are, the better. Vegetables also make an appearance, with celery and cucumber favourites for decoration. However, be careful if the bartender serves up something that has a turnip or large potato shoved in the glass. This isn't a cocktail, it's mulligatawny soup.

The type of ice used in cocktails also varies – with crushed ice, cracked ice, and normal blocks of ice. Look out for the unusual blue ice blocks. Look out for them, and then call the environmental health officer because these little blocks belong under the rim of a lavatory.

Many cocktails have frankly sexual names, such as Long Hard Screw Against the Wall, which provide hours of amusement when you ask the bartender for one. Remember, whatever your friends tell you, there is no cocktail called A Hard Smack in the Chops, so don't be in a hurry to ask for one.

The way you can distinguish a cocktail from a glass full of pink cat wormer is that the cocktail will have number of things adorning the glass – for example, a small umbrella, a swizzle stick and a slice of fruit. Avoid bartenders who are working to pay their way through art college. They tend to create overambitious tableaux that become a bit like the Chelsea Flower Show in a glass – great to look at, nightmare to drink.

At a certain stage, the amount of cocktail furniture in your glass seriously impedes your ability to drink it. Fortunately, there's generally a loop-the-loop straw which delivers your drink through five miles of coloured plastic piping. After one big suck, you can safely cross the bar, catch up with a friend and then return to your glass before the drink actually arrives at your mouth.

Finally, you know you've had enough cocktails when you need three people to get you safely off your bar stool and you feel exquisitely sophisticated but can't quite say it.

How to... tell jokes

Jokes are the chicken nuggets of conversation. You always think you want one, but generally they leave a bad taste in the mouth and bear very little resemblance to chicken.

The number of jokes you can remember is in inverse proportion to your natural charm and wit. The man with the joke for every occasion is the man you don't want to meet on any occasion. Most normal people can only ever remember one joke, and it's usually something fantastically unfunny like 'What do ghosts eat? Dreaded Wheat.'

Only a tiny handful of jokes are funny. Of those that are, there is a very high probability that you've heard them and a very low probability that they will be told well. That's why someone deciding to tell a joke is often a bit of a downer.

Generally, jokes are only told by men. That's because women prefer to communicate. Men have to stand up alone to be funny; women can do it sitting down with other people. Interrupting a man in mid-joke is extremely bad manners and is tantamount to interrupting his golf swing or his climactic moves in bed. A man in mid-joke is enjoying a brief moment when the world is not only listening to him but might even find him funny.

Pretending to laugh at a friend's joke is the closest most men get to faking orgasm. In order to give the laughter at the end any kind of credibility, it's best to start anticipating how enormously funny the punchline is going to be before you get there. Trying to laugh from cold will just sound like a car backfiring.

Men who tell jokes know deep inside that they're not funny. That's why they never stop at one joke. They tell them in packs of three so that if one goes flat they can always go straight into the next one. Sometimes they'll even end a joke by saying, 'That's not funny is it?' Don't be tempted to say, 'No, but consistent'. Beware men at work who have a daily joke delivered via their email. This is the character equivalent of a morning coffee to try and kick-start their personality.

When you see a joke coming, it's best to take rapid evasive action. If you're asked whether you've heard the one about the armadillo, immediately say 'yes'. Interestingly, they'll then tell you the whole joke minus the punchline to check if it's the exact same one about the armadillo. If they ask you how it goes, just make up a whole load of different armadillo scenarios until the whole armadillo subject becomes utterly unfunny.

How to... be confident

L ife is a confidence trick. Given enough confidence you can get away with anything. But confidence, like oil, is in short supply. If you have great reserves of it, you'll find you become widely liked and immensely wealthy without having to lift a finger. If you don't, you won't. It doesn't seem fair, but then confidence, like oil, is unfairly distributed.

Having confidence is like having an erection of the personality. Some people can sustain their confidence almost indefinitely; others have it for about twelve seconds before they revert to feeling small and embarrassed. Alcohol is Viagra for confidence. It helps you lose the three big confidence inhibitors: your self-doubt, your self-awareness, and your pathetically underpowered personality.

Real confidence is the unshakeable conviction that the universe is unfolding to your advantage. Confidence is a rich smoothie of optimism, charm and energy blended into a highly palatable mix. It may not have much substance but it's a meal in itself.

There are two types of confidence: natural confidence,

which comes from being brought up in a loving environment where your parents told you how wonderful you were every time you put felt-tip to paper; and artificial confidence, which comes from sniffing felt-tips.

Parties are the acid test of confidence, which is slightly odd as they're supposed to be where everybody relaxes and enjoys themselves. First, you have to have confidence to hold a party and believe people will turn up. Second, you have to have confidence to go to a party and talk to people you've never met before who will all be far more attractive and confident than you are. Third, you have to have confidence to leave a party when you realize that you are the most attractive and confident person there.

At an extreme level, martyrs are supremely confident in their cause because they're not afraid of death. This, however, is not the sort of confidence that makes you popular at parties. Not being afraid of life is what makes you popular at parties. Interestingly, martyrs often have a history of not being very popular at parties in their youth.

The worst thing that can happen to you, therefore, is to lose your confidence. One moment you have it and can charm the birds out of the trees. The next you've lost it and you're being shat on by every bird in the tree. It's a fine line to walk and there's no safety net.

Trying to get through life without confidence is 90 per cent harder than with confidence. But getting confidence when you haven't got it, or getting it back when you've lost it, is a trick that can only be pulled off with supreme confidence.

How to... do fancy dress

Most nations have a national costume; the English have fancy dress. When other nations get dressed up, they aim to look stylish and sophisticated. When the English get dressed up, they aim to look like Barney the dinosaur.

Saddest of all fancy dress is the gorilla suit. Everyone knows exactly what you are, so no one's going to ask, and no one knows who the hell you are, so they're not going to speak to you either. It's only fun to wear a suit like this at a party to which you haven't been invited.

Men choose themes such as tarts and vicars. This means all the women have to turn up dressed like prostitutes and the men have to reverse their collar. School uniform is another popular theme. For women this involves dressing up as the tartiest girl in class. For men it involves having a larger knot in their tie.

The best fancy-dress parties are where there is an imaginative theme with room for interpretation, such as 'earth, wind and fire'. You then get people who dress up as the lead guitarist from Mud, or a tin of baked beans, or a P45. When you're dressing up for this kind of theme you have to be careful not to be too clever. You could wear white shoes and white cap and a really nasty green and blue jumper to represent Earth as seen from space. But there's a good chance that people will just think that's how you normally look and strenuously avoid you.

At any given fancy-dress party there are three kinds of people: there are those who have made the effort and are wearing all sorts of cardboard, pins and kitchen utensils, and who spend the evening constantly rebuilding themselves; then there are the people who haven't made any effort at all, who tuck a trouser leg into a sock and pretend they're Long John Silver; finally, there are people who've made no effort but have spent a fortune in a theatrical costumier and come as Louis XIV. With this final lot, it's worth wilfully misinterpreting what they've come as all evening. Ask them whether it's school uniform, or a traffic warden or their normal pyjamas.

When you're in a last minute panic, it's amazing how versatile a black top and black trousers can be: with the simple addition of a sign you can become the Black Death, the Black Hole of Calcutta, black pudding, Black Sabbath, etc. An added bonus of the all-black approach is when you discover that no one else has come in fancy dress. You can then whip the sign off and just pretend you're a cool person who wears a lot of black.

How to... be popular

It's good to know that 90 per cent of men and women who were regarded as being the most popular at school are now in long-term psychiatric care under constant supervision. Sadly, this isn't true, but it's a lovely thought.

Most people want to be more popular. But really what most people want is to be more popular with the opposite sex. And, in fact, once they finally get a member of the opposite sex to share their sofa, pizza and chromosomes, they forget about popularity altogether and start to wear slippers.

The crucial question about popularity is whether you are popular with people you like or people you dislike. Many people have great swarms of friends, none of whom they like. These friends' only real purpose is to provide gossip so that they have something to talk about with the other friends they don't really like.

The best way to be popular is to treat other people as if they were already tremendously popular. Next time you accidentally bump into anorak Pete, treat him as if he were interesting and attractive. Inevitably, he will think you, too, are interesting and attractive, and you will be popular with him. Use this technique with care, otherwise you'll have anorak Pete shinning up your guttering late at night.

Don't confuse popularity with love. Money can buy you popularity, even if it's only with people who want your money. Similarly, don't confuse popularity with fame. Fame means you're popular with people you haven't even met. And if they worship you intensely from afar, it's going to be pretty frightening when you meet them in the flesh.

Alcohol is liquid fame. After two pints you not only think that people like you but you can begin to understand why, as you are obviously so witty, attractive and entertaining. A hangover is nature's way of reminding you how difficult it is to be permanently witty, attractive and entertaining.

If you seriously want to be popular, you need to start by getting out more. It's hard to be popular in the shed (although some people actually become more popular when they go there). You also need to be able to have a laugh, and the best place to start is with yourself. If the drinks and laughs are on you to start with, they'll both be on other people for the rest of the night.

The key to popularity changes with every generation: if you're a teenager, be cool and hang out; if you're in your twenties, be fun and party; and if you're any older, just be nice and keep the kettle on.

How to... dance

In clubs, men have a very formal dance which involves getting another beer and slumping lower in their chair. Eventually, after another eight drinks, the man gets up, selects a woman, and executes a movement that any right-minded referee would penalize as obstruction.

Some women get up on the floor and dance alone with their arms above their head. On no account try to dance with them, as they are obviously doing something intensely sensuous and won't want you suddenly grabbing them and spinning them. They're also likely to be a couple of swans short of a lake.

Rave dancing is pretty straightforward: you just take a little pill and the music tells you what to do. When you've finished dancing, you realize that you've been doing exactly the same movement for three hours, you're two stone lighter, and you've forgotten where you live.

At weddings and family parties, all generations can display their dancing skills. You can put on the Sex Pistols and the over-sixties will immediately start a nice little quickstep they perfected during the Blitz.

Parents who were alive in the sixties then recreate

some of the groovy moves with which they attempted to cash in on free love. These get the same kind of response they did then. Most people who are forced onto the floor opt for the traditional shuffling haddock routine where you step gingerly from one foot to the other and look intently at the floor as if you've just dropped 10p.

Sadly, the people who look most ridiculous on the dance floor are those who really enjoy dancing and are just full of an insane urge to move their body to Gloria Gaynor. They may be enjoying themselves but to everyone one else they look like Rumpelstiltskin.

Often you'll get an ugly couple who've been to dance classes. While everyone else is gently shimmying around, they're chucking each other over their heads and swinging each other round like they were in a throwing the hammer competition.

The only group that won't dance are the youngsters for whom the disco was specifically arranged. They are completely paralysed by coolness, and the songs played are never quite hip enough to overcome this. There's always one sad young man who has got it into his head that dancing involves barging into people. Nothing clears the dance floor faster than he does, and within seconds the old couple will be back doing their neat little Blitz quickstep.

MEN AND WOMEN

How to... write a personal ad

Abbreviations are very common in personal ads. The only one you really need to know is WLTM, which means the person in question likes a rare kind of country music only found on that particular American radio station. Strike them off your list immediately.

You'll also find N/S (non-smoking) and S/M (sado-masochist). Getting the two confused may make your first date extremely difficult, especially if you light up after being thrashed to within an inch of your life. That's when things could turn nasty.

Be very, very careful if you decide to meet someone who claims to have a GSOH, or great sense of humour. Really, this should be followed by the abbreviation IYTREMPSIF (If You Think Regurgitating Entire Monty Python Sketches Is Funny).

Generally, you should steer clear of abbreviations as they give the impression that you're a cheapskate trying to cut down the word count or that you've been in the dating game so long you now use a kind of desperate shorthand. Besides which, if your little ad is just a string of capital letters it rather gives the impression that you have the personality of a nappy bag (if you do, then fair enough).

Most people are quite coy about personal ads so try not to unwittingly identify yourself: 'heir to throne seeks like-minded plant', for example, would be a disaster. When describing yourself, try to steer clear of clichés: attractive only means your face is vaguely symmetrical; lively means you have a pulse; fun means you're not in tears all the time. On the other hand, don't go overboard with the descriptive stuff; 'picaresque Shavian sybarite' translates for most people as complete and utter knob.

Look carefully at what people say they want: 'friendship maybe more' means sex if I fancy you; 'country walks' means sex in haystack; 'romance' means sex after dinner; 'conversation' means sex on the sofa; 'travel' means sex on a ferry; 'laughter' means sex after joke; 'long evenings In' means sex after sex; 'long-term relationship' means sex after you've met my parents and established a rapport with my four children. Be very, very careful if someone just comes out with it and says they're after 'a strenuous physical relationship' as there is a very real danger that they might be a closet rambler.

Once you've spent time sifting through the one reply to your ad, you might decide you want to meet that particular someone in the flesh. Follow these few simple rules: meet in a public place (that doesn't mean your bedroom); tell a friend what you're doing (and they will tell everyone else they know); wear something recognizable (not your purple tweed jacket). And finally, if you've advertised in the *Guardian*, don't tell them you'll be carrying a rolled-up copy of the *Telegraph*.

How to... go on a date

Other than the army, the most horrific thing you can volunteer for in life is a date. There are two equally ghastly parts to the date: asking for the date, and the date itself. Remember, however bad you feel when someone turns you down for a date, the good news is that you don't then have to go on the date itself.

What makes a date so dreadful is the weight of expectation attached to it. There is every chance that you may meet your soulmate, get married, have children and be buried side by side. There is an equal chance that the person you meet will look as if they've already been buried for some time.

The hardest part of the date itself is the first line you say when you meet. If you can manage it, saying 'You look fantastic' is a great starter. Often, with nerves this can come out as 'You look fat', which can then take the shine off the rest of the evening.

Deciding what to wear on a first date takes approximately four times as long as the actual date itself. The golden rule is to wear what you feel most comfortable in, unless that is a fleecy romper suit. The time to buy a fancy new outfit is on the second date, when you know you've got an appreciative audience.

If you go out for dinner, remember that you should always split the bill. This means splitting in half, not working out exactly how many satay skewers she had and how that affects the final total. Never say to a woman that she ate a lot more than you and therefore should be paying a few quid extra because she's such a big eater.

Going to the cinema is a good idea on a first date if you find conversation difficult. However, it's worth bearing in mind that 8 per cent of arguments in established relationships are about what film to watch. If you insist on taking someone to a violent thriller, don't expect them to be whispering sweet nothings in your ear while someone on screen gets their face blown off.

Having a drink can help you relax. You should drink at a level that makes you feel increasingly sophisticated and your partner seem increasingly attractive as the evening wears on. When your sophistication meets their attractiveness, you have about a thirty-second window of opportunity to move in for the snog.

Generally, it's best to assume that a snog is completely off the menu for the first date. For men, this gives the impression that you're slightly cool and unimpressed, which is a good thing – especially if you grovelled embarrassingly to get the date in the first place.

How to... flatter

Effective flattery isn't difficult, especially for someone like you. The trick is to do it without the receiver noticing anything other than a warm feeling spreading through their body. There's a saying that flattery will get you anywhere. Be careful then, because you could tell someone how nice their hair looks and end up in Swindon.

It's very difficult to flatter someone on something they already know they're good at. There's no point going up to a legendary opera singer and saying, 'You've got a great voice'. They know it's good and they don't need you to tell them. Instead, tell them they've got one of the most attractive walks you've ever seen, strident yet sensuous, and they'll remember you every time they walk on stage.

Flattery needs to be applied with an implement. Laying it on with a trowel is sometimes the best policy. For example, you can tell any man that they are the most attractive, sexy human being ever and they will believe you even if there is a massive weight of evidence to the contrary.

Sometimes flattery should be applied like a stiletto knife, in that you should hardly feel it going in. Of course, you're wasting your time if you spend half an hour doing flattery so subtle that the other person goes away thinking you're actually rather dull.

The easiest way to flatter boring people is to pretend everything they say is interesting. Cock your head to one side, look intently at them, and say at regular intervals, 'That's fascinating!' Just be careful that the rest of your body doesn't go to sleep. You don't want all your invest-ment in flattery disrupted by killer pins and needles in your foot.

Try giving people credit for things they had no idea they had done. For example, in the office you could say, 'I love the way you said nothing in that meeting, Brian. That was a smart move.' Or in the middle of a meeting say, 'This idea came from Brenda', when Brenda has never had an idea in her life. If she queries this, tell her she was obviously implying the idea by the way her head was lolling.

The essence of flattery is to treat people better than they treat themselves. Some people love themselves to pieces, so advanced flattery techniques are required. Try telling them that they're just too hard on themselves. For people who love themselves, this would come as a worrying omission, so you can then become their con-sultant to increase their love for themselves.

Gauge how successful flattery has been by the response it gets: 'Do you really think so?' means they've accepted it; 'Thank you' means people know they're being flattered; 'Don't talk bollocks' means try again some other time.

How to... flirt

Flirting is vertical foreplay. Flirting happens when two people clearly have the right chemistry but before anyone gets their test tube out. Everyone loves flirting because when it happens it reminds you that you could be, you are, or you once were attractive to the opposite sex.

The eyes do a lot of the work in flirting. Eye contact is absolutely vital. No one's going to notice you flirting with them if you give all the appearance of being totally absorbed in a newspaper. On the other hand, you don't want to stare continuously at people without blinking. This gives the impression that you're either an off-duty optician or that you are about to stab them or both.

To flirt you need to look at someone slightly longer than normal, hold the gaze for 3.4 seconds, and then look away. It's then vital that you look back almost immediately. If the other person returns your gaze you know you're onto a winner. If the other person doesn't return your glance and has in fact started a new life in Canada, then it's probably a no-no.

Once you've established eye contact and the body

language is welcoming, you can move on to the 'accidental' touching. This is where you casually brush up against each other and maintain contact for longer than is strictly required by the laws of physics. With this stage, the inference is much heavier than the actual touch, and you would be wrong to squeeze the groin like a hooter (although this works with men).

Flirting also involves being fantastically rude to people in a flattering way. The fact that you can get away with it is a big sign from the other person that they like you. You're allowed to tell them that they're bossy, cheeky and saucy. You're not allowed to tell them that they're loud, aggressive or ugly.

The best flirters are people in happy stable relationships. Obviously, they don't flirt with each other, but they do have the confidence to flirt with other people. They also know through bitter experience the penalties of taking flirting too far and ending up in a happy stable relationship.

Some people are naturally flirtatious and everything they say or do seems like an invitation to carnal knowledge. Other people have no idea about flirting and have to go on special courses where they tell you to bat your eyelids. This does nothing for men, who need a more obvious signal like batting the buttocks, but it does have a curious stroboscopic effect on the batter and gives them the impression that they're in an old silent movie and actually flirting with Rudolph Valentino.

How to... attract men

Men have the sexual and emotional sophistication of a small dog, so attracting them is pretty straightforward. A whistle works very well to start with and then, when they've bounded over to you, simply rub their belly and they'll be yours for life. To maintain an optimum level of affection, you also have to make sure they're regularly fed and occasionally give them simple physical tasks so that they can assert their physical prowess. For the dog, this would be to fetch a stick; for a man, it would be opening a jam jar with a moderately stiff lid. Or you can test how keen your man is by seeing whether he'll fetch a stick.

Modern, enlightened man respects woman as his moral, economic and social equal; and the bigger her breasts, the more the respect. Breasts sympathetically arranged in an attractive display unit will be sufficient to attract any man with a pulse. That's the good news; the bad news is that they will also attract any man with a pulse.

It follows, therefore, that the difficult thing for women is to attract only those men whom she also finds attractive. Fortunately, when it comes to attracting a man, there are two powerful forces at work: a woman's appearance, and a man's ego. Remember, a man's ego can be expanded to fill any deficiencies in a woman's appearance.

The key is to unlock the power of gratuitous flattery. For example, if you can keep a straight face and tell the average man something like, 'You have a dangerously unsettling sexual aura', he will not only believe you immediately but will also believe it for the rest of his life against all evidence to the contrary.

Men like to project their energies and affections onto external things. A good way of attracting them is to flatter them on this external thing: take your pick from car, sound system, model railway, computer, shed, pigeon, medallion, yacht, or todger.

Theoretically, men like pin-ups but, practically, will settle for anything they can pin down. In fact, most men wouldn't know where to start when confronted with anything approaching a pin-up. Instead, men have a certain little something about women they find irresistibly attractive. You won't know you have this thing until you notice that the woman he leaves you for has the exact same thing as well.

Playing hard to get is a traditional way of pulling the man you want. Some men love the thrill of the chase, and your role should be that of hunt saboteur rather than just the fox. If a man has shown absolutely no initial interest, then playing hard to get will just make you look exceedingly odd. And that's when you find yourself becoming strangely attractive to men who are also exceedingly odd.

How to... attract women

The vital criterion for being successful with women is rock-solid confidence, and the only way to get rock-solid confidence is to be successful with women. So most men are stuffed from the word go. Women have a deep primal attraction to confidence because it tells them that you could go out and kill a woolly mammoth if you had to. Some women are attracted to anguished emotional cripples who can't commit because they think that given time all this will change. It won't, because that's how they attract women.

Women also like to have their own confidence boosted. You can do this by complimenting hair, weight, dress, eyes, shoes and clothing in any combination – for example, 'Those new shoes go well with your excellent haircut' works well; 'Your weight makes your shoes look big' doesn't.

Romance is important for women and is best when it is highly personal, intensely thoughtful, beautifully executed, and a complete surprise. Ideally, a romantic gesture will include many if not all of the following:

tissue paper, jewellery, keys, tickets, chocolate, baths, letters, thick white towelling dressing gowns.

Most women demand a good sense of humour in their man. Fortunately, most men develop a good sense of humour because they have to deal with women. Be warned that women don't think that belching the national anthem is funny. They're not even impressed with Stravinsky's *Rite of Spring*. What they want is a man who doesn't take himself too seriously. Women don't take men seriously in general, so they won't make an exception for you.

If you've got rock-solid confidence and a great sense of humour, you don't need to be great-looking. Of course, women would prefer you had all three, but then you'd almost certainly be gay and they'd be back to square one. What women do object to is embarrassing clothes. To a woman, you are basically a glorified accessory, and it's therefore very important that you don't clash or jar in any way.

You can have all of the above and still be a profound disappointment to women if you are a sloppy kisser. Kissing is important to women and shouldn't feel like you're rodding the drains or eating a watermelon. You should also concentrate on kissing because it gives you extra foreplay points and will go some way to meeting the impossible foreplay target that women set.

Being good at sex itself isn't really going to help you with seducing women as they're unlikely to take someone else's word for it, and by the time they find out you're rubbish it's too late and the wedding guests have gone.

How to... be romantic

Romance is emotional foreplay, and like all forms of foreplay demand outstrips supply. This isn't altogether surprising because in most cases women demand it and men are supposed to supply it. Romance isn't dead, it's just in a permanent vegetative state. When women's primary occupation was swooning, romance was all the rage. Now that sisters are doing it for them-selves, men have cut right back on romance because they wouldn't want to be accused of patronizing women. Which is a very handy excuse.

Men often think romance is getting what women want and giving it to them when they least expect it – for example, flowers at work, champagne on the beach, or breakfast in bed. But women also want shoes, and they wouldn't be very impressed if you whipped out a nice sensible pair that you'd chosen specially for them. So tread carefully.

Giving flowers is always a romantic gesture, but make sure it is flowers, not any old vegetable matter. Giving a single rose stem to someone is romantic, giving them a single turnip isn't. Although this might work in Norfolk.

Chocolates are romantic but chocolate isn't. Giving a women a 5 lb value bar of chocolate is a good way of saying you think she's a binge eater and won't get you very far. She'll still eat it, but you won't get the romance points. To be romantic, chocolates have to come in a packaging-to-chocolate ratio of roughly 10:1. When romance is over, women will buy their own chocolate in bulk with very little packaging.

Poetry is very romantic. If you can write your own, this is especially impressive – as long as you can do better than 'Roses are red, get into bed'. Generally, it's worth getting hold of a minor romantic poet, copying out large chunks, and changing the name to that of your beloved. No one's going to notice that you've changed Rosalind to Shania.

Taking women out to dinner can be romantic, but only if it's by candlelight. This allows them to eat more without being noticed and to look better because the only thing you can see is a six-inch flame in front of their face. Real romance involves tiny little attentive touches that show thoughtfulness, consideration and sensitivity on your part. Don't overdo this approach, as there's a real danger that you'll be so sensitive that you'll get gazumped by the man with the 10 lb of unwrapped chocolate.

How to... be suave

Since the dawn of time some men have believed that the secret of success with women and success in life in general is to be suave. There's an important difference between being suave and being cool – principally that being suave isn't cool. The basis of suavity is streamlining in personal grooming, social interaction and transportation.

Suave cars never have four doors and should preferably be convertible sports cars. It's impossible to be suave in a people carrier. Suave footwear mirrors the choice of car in that streamlining is also important. Slipons are therefore the shoes of choice for the suave. There is another option and that is suede. It's no coincidence that the word 'suede' is much like 'suave', because suede is the natural covering of the suave. A suave man wearing a lot of suede is elevated to the condition of being svelte, to which all the suave aspire.

Suave haircuts again tend towards the aerodynamic. It's extremely difficult to have big curly hair and pass yourself off as suave. Instead, you really need a slicked-back look which sweeps over the head and preferably ends in a rococo flourish on or very near the collar. Hair gel/glue should be applied in quantities sufficient to maintain maximum suavity at 60 mph with the hood of your sports car down.

Suavity in a man tends to focus around the neck. At one end of the spectrum is the medallion or tasteful St Christopher medal. At the other is the holy grail of suavity, the cravat. Both are difficult to carry off these days and are often substituted by the polo-neck sweater, preferably under a suede jacket.

It's the little touches that mark out the terminally suave: aftershave that would be subtle had fifteen times less of it been applied; large cufflinks on casual shirts; driving gloves; briefcases so slim they don't have an inside; long, over-elaborate sentences of such suavity that no one can remember a word you've said, ever.

Body language for the suave is dictated by the necessity of appearing to make very little effort to move. Suave men tend to lean on things a lot and walk in a gliding sort of way (much of this is because they're trying desperately to keep their suede slip-ons on their feet). For suave men, journeys that cannot be made on lounge carpets must be made in sports cars.

Suave men generally consider themselves to be enormously attractive to the opposite sex, which might be true if only anyone could work out exactly what the opposite sex to them was. Nevertheless, suave men still act as if they're sex on toast and as if their entire existence is enormously subtle and skilful foreplay of which all women are acutely aware. They stop thinking this in their late fifties when they discover that their only regular female companion is a suave-looking collie.

How to... be a good kisser

Before kissing, remove all foreign objects from the mouth, including pipes, cigarettes, pens, musical instruments and beards. If you are both wearing dental braces, do not attempt to kiss without the fire brigade in attendance with heavy cutting gear.

Make sure you clear the mouth of all food – remember you are kissing, not attempting to feed by regurgitation. Resist the temptation to be cute by passing your boiled sweet from your mouth to the mouth of your partner – one man's butterscotch is another woman's pineapple chunk.

Kissing is a specialized technique and should not be confused with any of the other functions of the mouth, such as blowing, sucking, chewing, spitting, gnawing, talking, or singing. Do not attempt to blow into somebody's mouth unless you think they may be having trouble breathing. If you feel the need to blow into something, try the ear, or a bassoon if there's one handy.

Unless you are Pavarotti, don't sing during kissing. Quite understandably, a lot of people are happy during kissing and inadvertently start humming – make sure it's

'The Very Thought of You' rather than 'The Dambusters March'. Biting and nibbling have their part to play in kissing, but go easy: a kiss is not a snack.

Obvious perhaps, but pre-kiss positioning is important. If you're not the same height, adjust yourself accordingly. Lying down is good, although this may give the wrong signal at the kissing stage. Now half-close your eyes, invade their body space, and make your lips look like an excitable monkey. If you're on the receiving end, this is not the time to blow your nose, turn away, or make a phone call. Instead, you need to replicate their actions and also tilt your head to one side to avoid nose clash. Clearly, don't tilt your head the same way as your partner, otherwise you'll end up ducking and diving like a pair of confused goldfish.

On contact with the opposition, kissing should commence with some gentle puckering. At this stage, it is not recommended that you uncoil your tongue like a fire hose and drop it down your partner's throat. Especially if it's a social kiss with a friend of your mother.

Once the tongue has been deployed, don't let it sit there doing nothing like a dishcloth on a draining board. What's required is bit of playful exploratory work which is high on wit and low on slobber. But don't overdo it – your partner should feel as though they've been kissed passionately, not had half an hour with a dental hygienist.

How to... be good in bed

Making love to somebody who thinks they're good in bed is like being on a graduate training scheme in a bank. Just when you're getting the hang of one position, they move you on to another. Changing position once you've started sex is actually dangerous and unnecessary. You wouldn't change driving position once a car was moving, so why on earth would you do it in bed? Best to stay where you are, safely strapped in.

Everyone has their favourite position for lovemaking. For most men, it is woman on top. For most women, it is woman on her side under duvet with man in airing cupboard hanging out laundry. There is a position after a furious bout of lovemaking where you lie totally still, side by side, in a kind of satisfied silence. This position is what married people do instead of a furious bout of lovemaking.

People who think they're good in bed often insist on dragging accessories into bed with them. You can be quietly enjoying yourself and suddenly you're expected to get busy with a food blender, strimmer or wallpaper table. If you're a woman and you don't want to accessorize, simply whisper 'later' into your lover's ear. Nine times out of ten there won't be a later.

For a man to be good in bed, the golden rule is not to get into bed. Instead, you have to spend a lot of time in restaurants and shops. This all counts as foreplay. Once you finally get down to it, the trick is not to get down to it and instead concentrate on kissing. Women like kissing and they're generally not happy unless they're coated head to foot in slobber.

Interestingly, for a woman to be good in bed, she only has to kiss a man lightly on the cheek. When the man tells his mates in the pub about it the next day, the woman will have suddenly become an absolute minx. It's very difficult for a woman to be good in bed when the man is rubbish. It's like being good at football but no one passing you the ball (as it were).

Talking about what you're going to do to each other when you get to bed can often be a very good form of foreplay. Run what you're going to say through your mind before you say it, and if you can only come up with one three-word sentence, saying it might actually be counterproductive.

Everyone knows about foreplay, but afterplay is equally important. This is where you kiss your partner, tell her how much you love her, and then wrench her entire duvet off.

LOVE AND MARRIAGE

How to... love

Most things in modern life have terms and conditions attached to them. The two exceptions are love and surrender, which both work best when they are unconditional. Love and surrender are very closely related, because when you fall in love you surrender yourself, your possessions and your sanity. True love is when you surrender yourself to another person. But two people should do this simultaneously, otherwise you're just getting yourself involved in complex power games with leather accessories.

Every generation has a love that dares not speak its name. Apart from this generation, which doesn't seem to have a love that keeps its mouth shut. Except, perhaps, for the love some men have for diesel-electric locomotives.

A great deal of the British capacity for love goes into animals, especially domestic ones. The animal you choose to love says a lot about you as a person. People who love dogs expect boundless love in return and generally have large, loud families. People who love cats prefer unrequited love and generally live quietly between a bookcase and a radio.

Guinea pigs are great pets to introduce young people to the basics of love in that they don't last very long, need constant messing out, and have long shaggy haircuts which mean it's difficult to tell the girls from the boys.

Men love women because they are the loveliest things on God's earth. Women love men because chocolate can't mow the lawn. Some men prefer to love other men. Equally, some women prefer to love other women. There's a word to describe this kind of behaviour. Love.

Everyone has an ideal lover. This can be dangerous because there's a big difference between the Brad Pitt of fantasy and the Arm Pitt of reality. But love, like body hair, turns up where you least expect it. The miracle of life is that, whoever you are, there really is somebody out there for you. The tragedy of life is that this person often lives in Swindon.

When love finishes, it feels really, really bad. On the bright side, you get possession of the entire duvet and a chance to read the paper before it is irretrievably damaged. Also, love is as perennial as the grass. Remember that there are many more fish in the sea. As long as you're happy to go out with a haddock.

Love and marriage used to go together like a horse and carriage. These days it's love and sex that go together. It is still possible to have one without the other, but only if you join a religious order. And if you just want love, get a pen pal.

How to... propose marriage

Short of saying, 'Genetically modify me, professor,' the quickest and most profound way of changing your life is to say to someone, 'Will you marry me?'

Men tempted to say this should be aware that what women actually hear is 'Do you want a wedding?' – a subtle but profound difference. The increasing number of women popping the question should be aware that what men hear is 'Do you want to stop seeing all the other women in the world apart from me and my mother?'

There are a range of answers you can expect after a proposal. 'Yes' is good, as is 'I'd love to, Ronald' (as long as you're called Ronald). 'No' can also be good, especially when accompanied by a tidal wave of relief. 'What the hell are you doing down there?' is not a positive response, and only the terminally optimistic would see encouraging signs in 'You are being held in a queue, but we value your enquiry'.

The worst response is 'Not yet' or 'Can I get back to you on that one?' The trick here is to keep asking them at regular monthly intervals and then suddenly stop for no reason. If they don't notice, find someone else, and if they do, find someone else anyway because you don't want someone who keeps you waiting for the rest of your life.

Generally, you can anticipate what sort of response you'll get; when you've been living with someone for years, they get very emotional at friends' weddings and know every frame of *Four Weddings and a Funeral*, you're quids in. If your intended gives regular seminars on 'Marriage: Catalyst for Patriarchal Exploitation', the little ring nestling in velvet might not do it for them.

The good thing about proposing marriage is that it puts a stop to the endless talking about commitment and worrying about the relationship implications of buying a double duvet. The bad thing is that making the proposal itself is like combining the fear of every date you've ever asked for, every loan you've ever begged for, and every exam result you've ever opened.

Going down on one knee is traditional, although you might as well go down on two knees because that's where you're going to be for the foreseeable future. The real stress starts after you've both said 'yes' – first, you test the relationship to destruction by arranging a wedding that will please both sets of parents, then you settle down to a state of permanent post-traumatic stress disorder – or marriage.

How to... give a best man's speech

Start your preparation several months before the big day. This way you'll either find out so much about the groom you'll want to turn him in to the police, or you'll find absolutely nothing and realize you've got to be funny about the Mother Teresa of Basingstoke.

The key thing is to know exactly who your audience is. They're the people in front of you. Seems obvious, but when you've had a few drinks you can end up doing your entire speech to the wedding cake.

The granny generation won't find anything you say funny or clever. The good news is that they won't hear a word you say anyway. The parents have probably just paid for the wedding so they won't want to be compared to the Addams Family. When you sit down, they'll want to know why that's so funny.

For teenagers, everything you say is totally crap and boring, so it's best to completely ignore them. Unless, of course, the bride and groom are teenagers. Young kids always get overexcited at weddings and are likely to run across the room in a cute way and punch you in the groin. It's the sincerest form of heckling.

Don't panic if your first joke is a bummer. Start to

panic if your twentieth joke is also a bummer, but remember it's never too late to turn your speech into a serious, reflective piece. Avoid being too clever with hecklers. When you say something like, 'It's hard to believe you were the best of a million sperm', that person is bound to be the vicar.

If in doubt, compliment a bridesmaid. When your really funny story about the groom and the chicken has provoked complete silence and horror, simply continue by saying, 'But I think we'd all agree just how wonderful little Hannah looks in her lovely dress'. During the applause you can scrub out the next three paragraphs about the chicken.

Remember, what you know about his love life and what his new wife knows are two completely different things. Concentrate on funny stories that happened a long, long time ago and where all the participants are now in Australia, in prison or dead. Preferably all three.

If you really have to tell the story about David super-gluing his genitals to a postbox, all his in-laws are going to think David's a plonker, all David's family will think you're a plonker, and the bride is going to think, 'Dave's got mutilated genitals'.

If you've done the preparation, you'll enjoy watching the video over and over again. If you haven't, then your speech will forever be on fast forward.

How to... be happily married

It's a sobering thought that almost two thirds of marriages in this country end happily. The bedrock for happiness in a marriage is for men to follow the simple rule that your wife is right and that you are sorry. For women, the trick is to let men have total authority over one thing. The choice is between the remote control, the road atlas or choice of slippers. Over everything else, men can assume they have control, but rule number one applies in practice.

Being faithful is more important in marriage than religion because you're more likely to be excommunicated if you transgress in a marriage. Sexual excitement may start to wane in a marriage and so you should think of all sorts of different ways to spice up the last few days of your honeymoon.

Marriage is for life, which these days can mean sixty or more years. A good way to fill in the time is by having six or seven children. This gives you something to do for the long middle years in a marriage when there's nothing on television.

People who wander around talking rubbish to themselves are generally considered slightly bonkers. In a marriage, you can do this all the time because there's someone in the other corner of the room making tea. This is what people refer to as companionship. This is the big thing in marriage when the sex, the children and the teeth have gone.

The best thing about marriage is the security and reassurance it offers. However bad things get in life, it is deeply reassuring and comforting to know that there is always someone worse off than yourself. Occasional arguments are good in a marriage because they can clear the air. If they also clear the furniture, you're probably taking them a bit too far.

One key to happy marriage is to realize that you can't change the person you've married. Ideally, you should realize this before you marry them and not march up the aisle with a massive mental 'to do' list. Just because you're married doesn't mean you can't do your own thing. Having your own interests is absolutely vital. Sport, travel, evenings in the pub, office outings should be actively encouraged, especially by wives.

When you get married, kindly old people tell you that marriage has to be worked on. Sadly, no one ever tells you what this work actually is and whether you can get a man in to do it for you. Generally, it's worth checking regularly how your other half feels the marriage is going. If the response comes in the form of a solicitor's letter, there may be something in the air.

How to... live together

You should only live with someone if you can't live without them. Living together in a couple is a highly unnatural activity. It starts as a desire not to have to go home after rampant sex and ends up as a bulk sock-purchasing policy.

Moving in together is possibly the most fraught time of living together. This is where the man discovers that 90 per cent of women's underpants are large grey freezer bags, and the woman discovers that men only have two pairs in total. You also have to start buying things together and you realize that there is no area of compromise between Lincoln biscuits and chocolate Hob Nobs.

In any couple, one person is tidy and the other is an absolute grub. The person who is tidy is grumpy because they think they're doing all the work and if they didn't clear up the whole house would be neck deep in filth. The grub is grumpy because they feel under continual crushing pressure to do all sorts of things that they would never dream of being important, such as keeping towels perpendicular to the towel rail.

Sometimes you may think you're living with someone but they've actually forgotten you're there. Telltale signs of this are when they continually switch lights off in the room where you're sitting, or regularly throw away personal items of yours simply because you're not currently using or wearing them.

Sharing a car is like sharing a house in miniature. For a tidy person, when you turn a corner the only noise should be the indicator ticking. For the absolute grub, it's a tide of rubbish slapping from one side of the car to the other. Never share with someone who leaves the car in gear, unless you enjoy starting your working day by stalling the car. And never share with someone who rips out the page of the atlas they need for any given trip.

Often, labour-saving devices in the home can be relationship-destroying devices. For example, what is the point of having a dishwasher if your partner can't fill it properly? Similarly, the washing machine ought to liberate couples to sip white wine and watch the sunset. In fact, it focuses attention on the fact that your partner doesn't know that a bra needs a cool wash otherwise the elastic goes. And if he's going to ruin your bras, then watching sunsets with wine is out.

The key to living together in a relationship is the same as in the diplomatic world: nothing keeps people together like a common enemy. That's why living together so often leads to children.

How to... have a tiff

The essential precondition for a tiff is to be tired. Combine this with a low blood-sugar level and just about anything you say or do will set off a tiff. When you're tired and hungry you're usually both in the kitchen desperately trying to get something to eat. A little instruction like 'Don't use that knife' said in the wrong tone can result in the knife in question sticking out of your back within seconds.

If you do have a tiff in the kitchen it's vital not to be the one who storms off to the bedroom because you will starve while your partner eats a good meal, feels better, and then sits in front of the television wondering where the hell you've got to.

Tiffs spring up from nowhere over issues of astonishing triviality – for example, the way you hang up your bath towel. You then have to be very careful that there's not a thermonuclear escalation into a deeply wounding psychological assault where things are said about weight, dress, haircut or mother-in-law. Tiffs blow over quickly, but the punishment for your remarks will be severe and will last a very long time.

Making up after tiffs is tricky as someone eventually has to say sorry. With stubborn people this sometimes never happens, and that's the last time you see them and their children and their children's children, ever. Normally, about three minutes after you've said all the hurtful things and an uneasy silence has descended, one person says, 'Look, Darren, I'm sorry' (doesn't have to be Darren obviously). Then Darren says, 'No, I'm sorry.' That's not the cue for you to say, 'I should bloody well think so!' Instead, you have to laugh, hug, and (if you want corking sex afterwards) cry.

The best excuse after a tiff is always to say that you were just very, very tired. Sadly, you can never use this excuse before a tiff, as saying 'I'm too tired to argue' has the same function as a starting pistol for most domestic arguments.

Lovers' tiffs are very amusing in that new lovers expect their little universe to be 100 per cent perfect. Therefore if you omit to kiss every single individual toe in turn, this is tantamount to a slap in the face and fully tiff-worthy. At the other extreme, couples who are married with children have heavily disguised tiffs. A man saying in a slightly strained way, 'I'm going to turn the compost,' is actually saying, 'And that's all you are, Jean, compost!' Of course, what happens is eventually he apologizes, they cry, make love, have another child, get overtired, and the tiffing continues.

How to... sulk

Sulking is emotional strike action. You still function as a human being but you work to rule. You must never agree to anything, you must only ever acquiesce to things. When someone asks if they should put the kettle on the correct answer is, 'If that's what you want do to'. That's because the underlying message of all sulking is that deep hurt is being felt because the other person is utterly selfish.

The big dilemma with sulking is whether you should slope off to another room to do it. Remember that out of sight is out of mind and they might forget that you're in a mountainous sulk. The best solution is to stay in the same room but pretend other people are not there.

Eye contact is a big no-no for sulkers, for two reasons. First, no eye contact is the clearest possible sign that a major sulk is under way. Second, if someone were to do anything funny or loving and you were to see it, you might inadvertently smile and the sulk would be irreparably damaged. It's a cast-iron rule that once you've unsulked you can't then re-sulk. It's like frozen food – once you've defrosted you can't then refrost.

Sulks can last anywhere between seven minutes and seven years. Teenagers are in an almost perpetual sulk because they are in a continual state of being misunderstood. Adults often manage to keep a sulk going for three or four days. When people are in a sulk they discover how much harder everyone else has to work to humour them. Some people enjoy this so much that they decide to become permanently grumpy.

The sulk, like the trifle, is a peculiarly British thing. That's because it's the form of emotional expression for people who don't know how to express themselves. The sulk says, 'I can't express myself, so I'm not going to express anything and you'll just have to guess what I would have expressed had I been able to express what I wanted to express'.

The sulkee then has to decide their response to the sulker. Ignoring the sulk is like ignoring the laundry basket – it'll keep building up until it gets very unpleasant indeed. You can ask what's troubling the sulker, but that's usually a little too casual. What's generally required to end a sulk is a mixture of complete attention, physical reassurance, brief subjection to verbal sarcasm, and then major admission of guilt and selfishness. As the air clears, it's absolutely vital not to say, 'That was a big sulk, wasn't it?' This is the quickest possible way of launching the world's largest, longest and deepest sulk.

How to... be sorry

A pologies are the old rubber tyres hung over the sides of huge egos to prevent damage when they rub up against each other. Apologies are all the rage these days. If you can't stomach an apology, you can just say you regret something. This is shorthand for 'I regret being in a situation where an apology is called for'. In fact, modern apologies don't mean that you apologize, you regret anything, or you are at fault. They're just the most polite way you can say, 'I dislike you intensely'.

An apology can be short-term pain for long-term gain. An apology, played right, can actually give you the upper hand. First of all, you've shown that you're big enough to admit you're wrong. Second, you've obviously had to take the pain, so you are in some way the victim and they are the brutal oppressor even though they're right on some slim technical grounds.

From this position, you can either counter-attack – 'I've said I'm sorry, what do you want, blood?' – or you can play the self-flagellation card – 'I'm wrong, I'm always wrong, I'm a worthless human being'. Or there's the philosophical approach: 'Factually you're right, but in moral terms I'm right'.

A breezy apology can be very annoying. Quickly saying, 'I'm sorry, what an idiot I am', denies the other person the chance to say, 'Apologize, you idiot'. Never repeat the fault in the apology. 'I'm sorry I called you a grumpy old trout and I want everyone here to know that'. If you're really sorry you can send a huge bunch of flowers and a little note saying, 'I'm sorry I made fun of your pollen allergy'.

Apologizing on behalf of other people is also a good tactic. Try arriving late at a meeting and saying 'I'm sorry you all arrived early.' Expert apologizers apologize even when it's obvious they're absolutely right. This gives the impression not that they're sorry, but that they're sorry for you, for being such a loser.

The only time it's really easy to say sorry is when saying sorry simply isn't enough. 'I'm sorry I blew your leg off' doesn't really do it. What's called for is a lifetime of remorse. And you can't just say, 'I've blown your leg off; I can feel a lifetime of remorse coming on'. You've got to feel it, live it and show it, even though, deep in your heart, you know it was really their leg at fault.

How to... be right all the time

Some people think that the easiest way to be right is to do and say absolutely nothing. The trouble is, the day before you die you realize you've got your whole life wrong. Another method of always being right is to live slightly behind the event horizon so that you can be permanently wise after the event.

Others never admit to being wrong even though all the evidence screams that they are. They're still right because conditions weren't right for them to be right and had all the facts been utterly different they would have been totally right. (Take your pick from most major political, social and health fashions of the century.)

On the other hand, it's no good being completely right about something no one gives a monkey's about. No one cares that you're completely right about the height of a gasometer.

If you're going to be right about everything (and it's astonishing how many people are), the simplest way is to decide from the outset that being wrong is not an option for you. Once you've got this settled, you develop two attendant medical conditions, jaundiced eye and sieve ear, which combine to give the impression that everything in life supports whatever you decide is right.

If you don't have the head of a pig, an easier way to be right is to have infinitely flexible opinions so that you can start a sentence with one opinion and finish it with another. However, if you don't have firm opinions you forsake the pleasure of saying 'I told you so' or 'You really cacked that one up, Bernie'.

Being right all the time isn't easy, as right and wrong keep changing. For example, it is now right to wear corduroy trousers. That doesn't mean you were right to wear them non-stop for the last twenty years in the teeth of opposition from friends, family and fashion editors.

Don't ever try to prove someone who's always right wrong. Even when you think you've done it, thirty years later they'll call you out of the blue and tell you that they were right about that gasometer all along.

The reason the final judgement is such an appealing idea to many is that those who live with the always-right expect them to be proved wrong and those who are always right expect to have this confirmed. The final judgement will decide once and for all who is right. Unless, of course, they get it wrong.

How to... control the duvet

In the modern world, the phrase 'Who's wearing the trousers?' should be updated to 'Who's hogging the duvet?' Control of the duvet is the front line in the struggle for power in any bed-based relationship.

Moving very slowly and steadily into the middle of the bed gets you more of the crucial central duvet. This can be done with any number of ruses, the most common one being cuddling. It's great having a cuddle in the middle of the bed, but sooner or later someone has to roll away. Make sure your partner does the rolling by giving them a playful shove in the right direction.

The holy grail of duvet management is if you can somehow secure it to prevent slippage. If there is a little bit of spare duvet, you can tuck it under your body and create a tight sleeping-bag effect around you. With a normal-size duvet, this tight sleeping-bag effect generally creates a loose outdoor effect for your partner, so don't expect it to last.

A more desperate approach uses the buttons on the bottom of your duvet. You can swivel the duvet round so that the button end is alongside you and then button the duvet into your pyjamas. This will prevent casual driftage and also, in the event of a massive tug by your partner, will make sure you stay attached to the duvet wherever it ends up.

A nasty, underhand method of duvet retention is used where the duvet cover is bigger than the duvet itself. In this case, there is always a flappy bit of cover that doesn't actually have any duvet inside. Position this flappy, empty bit over your partner and the plump, well-stuffed bit over yourself.

Getting up to go to the loo is an admission of defeat in the duvet wars. All the duvet and warm air you've patiently acquired immediately revert to your partner. When you get back, you'll be left with the flappy, empty cover. You then have to start something called duvet-winching.

During the myriad little bodily adjustments one makes before getting comfortable, a tiny inch or two of duvet is winched away from your partner and around your body. You can attempt to cover your winching by little sighing noises or random questions, like 'Should we get married?' In this way, your partner will think the cold chill they're suddenly feeling is some kind of physical reaction to the question.

The trick with duvet-winching is to keeping doing it until your partner is a little, shivering, naked rat. Remember, if they love you, they'll forgive you.